Janet T. Spence

University of Texas at Austin

Workbook to accompany Elementary Statistics
fifth edition

Janet T. Spence
John W. Cotton
Benton J. Underwood
Carl P. Duncan

Prentice Hall, Englewood Cliffs, New Jersey 07632

Editorial/production supervision and interior design: **Ben Smith**
Manufacturing buyer: **Bob Anderson**

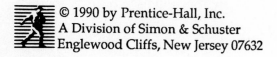
Printed in the United States of America

10 9 8 7 6 5 4 3

ISBN   0-13-260134-6

Prentice-Hall International (UK) Limited, *London*
Prentice-Hall of Australia Pty. Limited, *Sydney*
Prentice-Hall Canada Inc., *Toronto*
Prentice-Hall Hispanoamericana, S.A, *Mexico*
Prentice-Hall of India Private Limited, *New Delhi*
Prentice-Hall of Japan, Inc., *Tokyo*
Simon & Schuster Asia Pte. Ltd., *Singapore*
Editora Prentice-Hall do Brasil, Ltda., *Rio de Janeiro*

Contents

Section A

To the Student:
How to Use
the *Workbook*

The *Workbook to Accompany Elementary Statistics* contains several types of materials that supplement the textbook. These include sets of problems keyed to each of the 16 text chapters and also a series of special reviews that integrate topics in several chapters. The major features of the *Workbook* are briefly described below.

1.   Chapter Problems

   (a) List of terms and symbols

   Each set of problems starts with a list of the major terms and symbols that occur in the chapter. You should review them to make sure you know their meaning, referring to the textbook when you don't know. (Definitions of most of these terms and symbols can be found at the end of the chapter.) These terms and symbols are much like the lists of words you are expected to memorize in foreign language courses. Without knowing its basic vocabulary, you will have problems comprehending the "language" of statistics.

   (b) Short-answer questions

   Next you will find a series of items that require you to supply short answers. These items allow you to review and test your understanding of the major points covered in the chapter.

   (c) Other objective questions

   For some chapters these short-answer questions are followed by multiple-choice or matching questions that further test your understanding of major concepts.

   (d) Simple computational problems

   In chapters describing statistics that require calculation, simple problems are presented to give you practice in using the proper computational procedures. Only a few numbers, small in size, are used in these problems in order to emphasize the procedures by minimizing the amount of routine arithmetic required.

Answers to the items in each of these sections are supplied in the *Workbook* . You should check your answers *immediately* for accuracy. When you have not answered correctly, try to figure out where you went wrong and reread relevant parts of the text. Redo your calculations when necessary.

(e) Further exercises

The problem set for each chapter (except the first) concludes with a series of further exercises. This subsection is made up of thought questions designed to advance your understanding of various statistical concepts and of more complex computational problems that often describe a specific hypothetical research study and employ the kinds of data you might actually obtain in such a study. You will find that a calculator is very useful in solving the problems requiring computation, as explained in the text.

The answers to these exercises are *not* contained in the *Workbook*. However, your instructor may choose to give you a copy of the booklet with the answers so you can check your own work or get an idea about how to get started on problems you find confusing.

2. Supplementary Material

(a) Arithmetic review

The second section (B) of the *Workbook* contains an arithmetic review that lists common mathematical symbols you will encounter in the text and goes over the basic rules of arithmetic and simple algebra. You are advised to glance over the symbols to make sure you are familiar with them. Those of you who are out of practice or are uncomfortable with numbers should also go over the basic arithmetic rules and solve the practice problems. You need to understand these rules even when you use a calculator to perform the actual numerical operations called for in computational problems.

(b) Special reviews

Special reviews that integrate material in several chapters are found in the latter portions of the *Workbook*. The final section contains a decision tree, reproduced from Chapter 16 of the text. The decision tree allows you to select the appropriate statistical test to apply to a specific set of data that will allow you to answer the research question posed by the study. Learning what statistical techniques are appropriate in particular situations is as important as learning how to apply the techniques to actual data.

3. Formulas

At the end of the *Workbook* you will find reproduced the summary of useful formulas printed on the end papers of the text and the full numbered list of formulas found in Appendix II of the text. The formula numbers correspond to those in the text and the page number at the right of each formula indicates where in the text it may be found.

You will notice that the pages of the *Workbook* are perforated so that they may easily be torn out. Rather than flipping pages back and forth when you are working on problems in the text or the *Workbook*, you may find it convenient to detach the pages containing the formula lists from the *Workbook* and have them in front of you as you work.

Your instructor may ask you to tear out and hand in your solutions to the exercises in various sections and return them to you after your answers have been checked. You will notice that the *Workbook* pages have been punched so that they can be placed in a three-ring loose-leaf notebook. You might keep the *Workbook* materials that are torn out and returned in proper order in a notebook or even more simply, by metal rings available at your bookstore.

Section B

Arithmetic Review

The calculations required for solution of the problems contained in the text and in the *Workbook* call upon nothing more complicated than basic arithmetic operation and an occasional bit of simple algebra. Your arithmetic labors can also be simplified by the use of a calculator. Nonetheless, knowledge of arithmetic procedures is necessary and you may be out of practice.

For those of you whose skills are a bit rusty, this section provides a review of common mathematical symbols and some of the fundamentals of arithmetic and algebra. Also provided are a series of problems and the answers to them. It would be wise to look over the review material and then to solve as many problems as you require to master the rules involved.

MATHEMATICAL SYMBOLS

Listed below are a series of symbols that are used to indicate certain relationships or the arithmetic operations that are to be performed. The symbols X and Y are used as general expressions for numerical quantities.

Additional symbols are to be found in the text. Their meanings are explained when they first occur.

Symbols	Definitions
X + Y	Add X and Y.
X − Y	Subtract Y from X.

$X \div Y$ X/Y $\dfrac{X}{Y}$	Each of these expressions specifies that X is to be divided by Y. The number that is to be divided (X in these examples) is called the *dividend* and the number by which the dividend is to be divided is called the *divisor*. The result is called the *quotient*.
$X \times Y$ $X \cdot Y$ $X(Y)$ $(X)(Y)$	Multiply X by Y. The result is called the *product*.
Σ	Greek capital letter sigma, which indicates that a series of quantities that follow are to be summed (see p. 50 of the text for further explanation).
N	The number of quantities in a group or series of quantities.
$\sqrt{X}$	Square root of X.
X^2	The exponent 2 indicates that X is to be squared or raised to the 2nd power.
X^n	The exponent n indicates that X is to be raised to the nth power by multiplying X by itself n times (e.g., X^2, X^3, X^4).
$\lvert X \rvert$	Absolute value of X, that is, the value of X ignoring its plus or minus sign.
$X \neq Y$	X is unequal to Y.
$X < Y$	X is less than Y.
$X > Y$	X is greater than Y.

MATHEMATICAL OPERATIONS

Some of the fundamental rules of arithmetic and simple algebra are reviewed in this section.

Decimals

1. Addition and subtraction
   In adding and subtracting decimals, arrange the numbers in a column, keeping the decimal points in the numbers and the answer in a straight, vertical line.

   Examples:

Addition	Subtraction
.53	9.80
1.64	− 6.31
2.17	3.49

2. Multiplication
   The numbers are first multiplied as if they were whole numbers. The number of decimal places in the product is determined by adding up the number of decimal places in the two numbers being multiplied. Counting from the right, place the decimal point in the appropriate place.

2

Examples:

$$4.32$$
$$\times 1.63$$
$$1296$$
$$2592$$
$$432$$
$$70416$$

$$6.84$$
$$\times 2.3$$
$$2052$$
$$1368$$
$$15732$$

Decimals:

$$2 + 2 = 4 \quad 2 + 1 = 3$$

Answer:

$$7.0416 \qquad 15.732$$

3. Division
    Multiply both the divisor and the dividend by the multiple of 10 (10, 100, 1000, etc.) that will remove the decimals from *both* numbers. Then divide these two numbers as usual.

Examples:

$$\frac{8.3}{2.5} \times \frac{10}{10} = \frac{83}{25} = 3.32 \qquad \frac{16.3}{5.41} \times \frac{100}{100} = \frac{1630}{541} = 3.013$$

$$\frac{.465}{1.86} \times \frac{1000}{1000} = \frac{465}{1860} = .25$$

Note: The same whole numbers will result if, in the number with the largest number of decimals, the decimal point is moved enough places to the right to make it a whole number and then moved the same number of places to the right in the other number. (Add zeroes to the other number, as appropriate.)

Example:

In the example .465/1.86 above, move the decimals three places to the right, thus giving 465/1860).

Practice Problems

Find the answers to the following problems.

(a) 6.12 + 3.84   _____

(b) 4.36 + 2.01 + 3.54   _____

3

(c) 18.67 – 9.15 _____

(d) 5.99 – 1.06 _____

(e) (1.4) (.2) _____

(f) (2.21) (.3) _____

(g) (.32) (.44) _____

(h) 8.42/.2 _____

(i) 9.363/.3 _____

(j) 16.84/8 _____

Answers

(a) 9.96   (b) 9.91   (c) 9.52   (d) 4.93   (e) .28   (f) .663   (g) .1408   (h) 42.1

(i) 31.21   (j) 2.105

Fractions

The top number in a fraction is called the *numerator* and the bottom number is called the *denominator*. For example, in the fraction 3/16, 3 is the numerator and 16 is the denominator.
There are two basic methods for working with fractions.

1. Convert each fraction to a decimal by dividing the numerator by the denominator and then proceed as described in the section above on decimals.

Examples:

$$3/4 + 1/8 = .75 + .125 = .875$$
$$16/7 – 12/8 = 2.29 – 1.5 = .79$$
$$10/6 \times 5/4 = 1.67 \times 1.25 = 2.09$$
$$5/6 \div 1/2 = .83 \div .50 = 1.66$$

2. Work directly with the fractions, using the following rules.
    (a) Addition and Subtraction. Convert the fractions to ones with the smallest common denominator, add or subtract the numerators of the converted fractions, and place the sum over the common denominator.

Example:

$$1/4 + 1/2 + 5/8 = 2/8 + 4/8 + 5/8 = 11/8$$

(b) Multiplication. Multiply the numerators of the fractions together to obtain the numerator of the answer and multiply the denominators together to obtain the denominator of the answer.

4

Example:

$$(1/2)\,(2/3)\,(2/5) = \frac{1 \cdot 2 \cdot 2}{2 \cdot 3 \cdot 5} = \frac{4}{30}$$

(c) Division. Invert the divisor (the number you are dividing by) and then multiply the two fractions, as in (b) above.

Example:

$$3/4 \div 1/2 = (3/4)\,(2/1) = 6/4$$

If the fractions are small in size and number, it is usually simpler to deal with them directly. If not, it is typically more convenient to convert them to decimals and to solve the problem using the decimals.

Practice Problems

In finding the answers, work directly with the fractions rather than converting them to decimals. Leave the answers in fractional form.

(a) 1/2 + 2/3 + 5/6 _____

(b) 3/4 + 3/16 + 5/8 _____

(c) 9/10 − 2/5 _____

(d) 5/8 − 1/3 _____

(e) (2/3) (1/5) _____

(f) (1/4) (3/5) (5/6) _____

(g) (1/3) / (4/5) _____

(h) (3/4) / (1/2) _____

(i) (4/10) / (2/3) _____

Answers

(a) 12/6   (b) 25/16   (c) 5/10   (d) 7/24   (e) 2/15   (f) 15/120   (g) 5/12   (h) 6/4
(i) 12/20

Proportions and Percents

1. Proportions
    A whole may be divided into two or more parts. Each part may be described as a *proportion* of the whole, the proportion being obtained by dividing the size of the part by the size of the whole.

Example:

In a class of 58 students, 10 are freshmen, 27 are sophomores, 12 are juniors, and 9 are seniors. The proportions at each year level are 10/58 or .17, 27/58 or .47, 12/58 or .21, and 9/58 or .16.

The sum of the proportions always adds up to 1.00 (except for rounding errors when proportions are expressed as decimals). Thus, in the example above

$$\frac{10 + 27 + 12 + 9}{58} = \frac{58}{58} = 1.00$$

or

.17 + .47 + .21 + .16 = 1.01 (Note the slight rounding error)

2. Percents

(a) The *percentage* of the whole represented by each part is found by multiplying the part's proportion by 100. Except for rounding errors, the sum of the percentages always adds up to 100.

Example:

In the class of 58 students, 26 are women and 32 are men. The proportion of women is thus 26/58 and the percentage of women is:

(26/58) (100) = 45%

Similarly, the percentage of men is:

(32/58) (100) = 55%

and

45 + 55 = 100%

(b) When the number of cases corresponding to a specified percent is to be computed, the process is reversed: the total number making up the whole is multiplied by the specified percent and the product divided by 100:

$$\text{Desired Number} = \frac{(\text{Total number}) (\text{Percent})}{100}$$

Example:

60% of a group of 48 individuals is (48) (60)/100 = 2880/100 = 28.80.

6

Practice Problems

1. In a group of 50 individuals, 26 are married and 24 are unmarried.

    (a) What proportion is married? _____

    (b) What proportion is unmarried? _____

    (c) The sum of the two proportions is what? _____

2. The 200 passengers of a plane are given a choice of chicken, beef, or fish for the main course of their dinner. Sixty-eight chose chicken, 82 chose beef, and the rest chose fish.

    What proportion chose each? _____

3.   75 is what percent of 150? _____

4.   20 is what percent of 85? _____

5.   104 is what percent of 300? _____

6.   20% of 200 is what? _____

7.   75% of 50 is what? _____

Answers

1. (a) .52   (b) .48   (c) 1.00   2. .34, .41, and .25   3. 50%   4. 23.5%   5. 34.7%
6. 40   7. 37.5

Negative Numbers

1. Addition
    (a) When all numbers are negative, add the numbers and attach a negative sign to the sum.

    Example:

    $$(-4) + (-8) + (-2) = -14$$

    (b) When two numbers that differ in sign are to be added, *subtract* the *absolute* value of the larger number from the *absolute* value of the smaller number and attach the sign of the larger number to the result.

    Example:

    $$(-16) + (7) = -9 \qquad (41) + (-30) = 11$$

    (c) When a mixed series of positive and negative numbers is to be added, the rules described in (a) and (b) may be successively applied. When the series is large, it is more convenient to add the positive numbers and the negative numbers separately and then add the two sums as in (b).

7

Example:

$$\text{Add: } (-4) + (6) + (-8) + (-2) + (2) + (3).$$

$$(-4) + (-8) + (-2) = -14; \quad (6) + (2) + (3) = 11$$
$$(-14) + (11) = -3$$

2. Subtraction

When a negative number is to be subtracted from another number, change the number to be subtracted to a positive number and *add.* If the other number is positive, add the two positive numbers as usual. If the other number is negative, use rule 1(b) above for adding a positive and a negative number.

Examples:

$$(15) - (-4) = (15) + (4) = 19$$
$$(-20) - (-6) = (-20) + (6) = -14$$
$$(-3) - (-8) = (8) + (-3) = 5$$

Practice Problems

Find the answers to the following problems.

(a) $(-8) + (-7) + (-3)$ _____

(b) $(-6) + (-12) + (-4)$ _____

(c) $(-12) + 18$ _____

(d) $26 + (-4)$ _____

(e) $10 + (-40)$ _____

(f) $10 + (-3) + (-41) - (-23) + (-16)$ _____

(g) $(-4) + 2 + (-1) + 13 + 4 + (-8)$ _____

(h) $20 - (-4)$ _____

(i) $5 - (-3)$ _____

(j) $2 - (-8)$ _____

(k) $(-16) - (-12)$ _____

(l) $(-9) - (-15)$ _____

Answers

(a) –18   (b) –22   (c) 6   (d) 22   (e) –30   (f) –27   (g) 6   (h) 24   (i) 8
(j) 10   (k) –4   (l) 6

Exponents

An exponent indicates how many times a quantity is to be multiplied by itself (also expressed as the power to which the quantity is to be raised). Thus, in the expression X^2, the exponent appearing at the upper right indicates that X is to be squared (by multiplying X by X) or raised to the second power. Similarly, in the expression X^3, the exponent 3 indicates that X is to be cubed (X x X x X) or raised to the third power; in the expression X^4, the exponent 4 indicates that X is raised to the fourth power (X x X x X x X), and so forth.

Mixed Operations

Many expressions contain a mixture of addition, subtraction, multiplication, and division. Certain rules govern the order in which these operations are to be conducted. Three rules are sufficient to cover the kinds of expressions you will encounter in the text.

1. Expressions involving multiplication and addition and/or subtraction
    The basic rule is that multiplication is performed first.

    Example:

    In the expression

    $$3 \times 5 + 6 + 2 \times 4$$

    the terms 3 x 5 and 2 x 4 must be obtained before the addition is carried out:

    $$3 \times 5 = 15, \text{ and } 2 \times 4 = 8, \text{ and}$$
    $$15 + 6 + 8 = 29$$

2. Expressions involving parentheses and brackets
    The operations within each set of parentheses are performed first, then the operations within each set of brackets, and then the remaining operations.

    Example:

    $$(4 + 5)^2 - (3 + 2)^2 = 9^2 - 5^2 = 81 - 25 = 56$$
    $$[5 (3 + 1)/2] - 4 = [5 (4)/2] - 4 = 10 - 4 = 6$$

    Exception: In expressions of the form A (B + C), the answer may be found either by adding B and C and then multiplying the sum by A, or by first finding (A) (B) and (A) (C) and then adding the two products. Thus

    $$A (B + C) = AB + AC$$

    Example:

    $$5 (4 + 2) = 5 (6) = 20 + 10 = 30$$

    Similarly, in expressions of the form A (B – C)

    $$A (B - C) = AB - AC$$

3. Expressions involving division

The operations in the numerator and in the denominator are performed separately and then the division is performed.

Example:

$$\frac{(10 + 3)^2}{4 + 5 + 2} = \frac{13^2}{11} = \frac{169}{11} = 15.36$$

Practice Problems

(a) $(9 + 3)^2 + (4 + 2)^2$ _____

(b) $(10 - 5) + (8 - 6)$ _____

(c) $\dfrac{(7 + 6) - (3 + 2)}{4 + 5}$ _____

(d) $\dfrac{[(8 + 2)^2 / 5] - 6}{3 + 4}$ _____

Answers

(a) 180   (b) 7   (c) 8/9   (d) $14/7 = 2$

Solution of Algebraic Problems

In solving a problem in which there is one unknown, the unknown quantity is placed on one side of the equal sign and the remaining quantities on the other. Rearrangement of the formula may be required to isolate the unknown, using the following rules.

1. The same quantity can be added to or subtracted from both sides of the equation without changing the value of the unknown. This in turn implies that a term may be transposed from one side of the equation to the other simply by changing the sign of the transposed term.

Examples:

In the expression

$$A = B + C$$

(a) Transpose C:

$$A - C = B$$

which is the equivalent of subtracting C from both sides:

$$A - C = B + C - C = B$$

10

(b) Transpose B:

$$A - B = C$$

(c) Transpose both B and C:

$$A - B - C = 0$$

or

$$A - (B + C) = 0$$

Similarly, in the expression

$$A = B - C$$

(a) $A + C = B$

(b) $C = B - A$

(c) $A + C - B = 0$

2. Both sides of the equation can be multiplied or divided by the same number without changing the value of the unknown.

Examples:

Multiply both sides of the equation $A = \dfrac{B}{C}$ by C:

$$A\,(C) = \dfrac{B}{C}\,(C)$$

$$A\,(C) = B$$

Divide both sides of the equation $C = (A)\,(B)$ by B:

$$\dfrac{C}{B} = \dfrac{(A)\,(B)}{B} = A$$

Practice Problems

In each of the following, solve for X. (To do so, you must rearrange the equation so that X is alone on one side of the equal sign.)

(a) $5 = X + 4$ _____

(b) $6 + 2 = X/2$ _____

(c) $6X = 18$ _____

(d) $(X + 4)/3 = 4$ _____

(e) $16 = X^2/4$ _____

(f) $2X/4 = 5$ _____

11

Answers

(a) $X = 5 - 4 = 1$ (b) $X = 2(6 + 2) = 16$ (c) $X = 18/6 = 3$ (d) $X = (4)(3) - 4 = 8$

(e) $X = \sqrt{(16)(4)} = 8$ (f) $X = (5)(4)/2 = 10$

Section C

Problems for Chapter 1:
Statistics:
What It's About

I. TERMS AND SYMBOLS TO REVIEW

Descriptive statistics   Sample statistic

Inferential statistics   Numerical data

Population   Magnitude data

Sample   Discrete variables

Random sample   Continuous variables

Randomization   Rank-order or ordinal data

Matched pairs   Categorical or nominal data

Population parameter   Mutually exclusive categories

II. SHORT-ANSWER QUESTIONS

1. All the members of a group who have at least one specified characteristic in common

    constitute a _____.

2. A sample is defined as _____

    _____.

3. When a sample is to be selected so that conclusions can be drawn about a population, many methods can be used. The aim is to select a sample that is _____ of the population.

4. A random sample is one selected in such a way that (a) _____

_____

and (b) _____.

5. Fifty *different* individuals are selected consecutively at random from a population of 1000. This is called sampling _____ replacement.

6. The 100 members of a population are each assigned a different number from 1 through 100. Select a random sample of 5 individuals without replacement, using the page of random numbers in Table A, Appendix III of the text. Start with the 11th number in the third column (21715). The numbers of the 5 individuals are ____ , ___ , ___ , ___ , ___.

7. When two or more samples are randomly drawn from a population, the samples are *independent*. This means _____

_____

_____.

8. In an experiment in which participants are to be tested under two or more conditions, the experimenter attempts to select samples that are initially comparable. Comparability means that _____

_____.

9. Members of a pool of individuals who serve in an experiment with two or more groups can be assigned at random to experimental conditions. This method produces what are known as (a) _____ samples and samples that are (independent or nonindependent) (b) _____.

10. Testing the same individual under all experimental conditions produces (a) _____ that constitute (independent or nonindependent) (b) _____ samples.

11. When matched pairs, each of which contains two different individuals, are employed in a two-group experiment, the members of each pair have been selected by _____

_____.

12. A number representing a property of a population of individuals is known as a population (a) _____ and a number representing a property of a sample is known as a sample (b) _____. The symbols used to indicate population values are typically (c) _____ and the symbols used to indicate sample values are typically (d) _____.

13. With numerical data, the question that is asked about the property of each individual is

_____.

14. The difference between measurable properties that are continuous and those that are discrete

is _____

_____

_____.

15. In a footrace, George came in first, John came in second, and so forth. This is an example of

_____ data.

16. When individuals in a group are to be assigned to a set of categories, the question asked about

each individual with respect to each category is whether _____

_____.

17. After members of a group have been assigned to categories, the results for the group are

obtained by _____.

18. In a set of mutually exclusive categories, each individual can be assigned to

(a) _____ category, whereas in a set of nonmutually exclusive categories,

each individual may be assigned to (b) _____.

19. Categorical data are also known as _____ data.

Answers

1. population   2. a subset of individuals from a population that takes any number less than the total number in the population   3. representative   4. (a) every individual has an equal probability of being selected   (b) every possible sample of a given size has an equal probability of being selected   5. without   6. 21, 72, 96, 68, 65   7. selection of members of one sample does not influence which individuals remaining in the pool are selected in a subsequently drawn sample   8. if the samples were all tested under the same experimental conditions, they would not perform differently   9. (a) randomized   (b) independent   10. (a) matched pairs (b) nonindependent   11. matching the pair of individuals on one or more relevant properties (i.e., properties that influence performance on the experimental task)   12. (a) parameter (b) statistic   (c) Greek letters   (d) regular letters   13. how much of the property does the individual exhibit?   14. with continuous properties, individuals may fall any place along the scale of values between the upper and lower limits imposed by nature; with discrete properties, individuals may fall only at certain points along the scale of values   15. rank-order
16. the individual does or does not exhibit the property specified by the category
17. counting the number of individuals in each category   18. (a) one and only one   (b) more than one category   19. nominal

III.   MATCHING QUESTIONS

For each of the following, indicate which type of data is being described.

   (a) numerical   (b) rank order   (c) mutually exclusive categories
   (d) nonmutually exclusive categories

nominal (1.) A naturalist determines the number of sparrows, robins, and blue jays that appear at a feeding station during an 8-hour period.

ordinal (2.) A critic's ordered list of the best 10 movies of the past year.

ratio (3.) In a test of motor skills, the time taken to sort a set of objects into bins.

nominal (4.) Classification into type of birth defects exhibited by all children born in City Hospital over the past 24 months.

Answers

1. (c)   2. (b)   3. (a)   4. (d)

For each of the following, indicate what type of sampling procedure was employed.

    (a) random   (b) randomized   (c) matched pairs

_____ 1. Individuals participating in a study of leader-follower behavior work together in pairs on a task. One member is chosen as the leader and the other as the follower by a flip of a coin.

_____ 2. Hospitalized schizophrenics are tested on a reasoning task. Patients with medical problems, each similar in age and education to one of the schizophrenics, are given the same task.

_____ 3. In a survey of student attitudes at a particular college, every tenth student in the Student Directory is sent a survey booklet.

Answers

1. (b)   2. (c)   3. (a)

16

Section D

Problems for Chapter 2:
Frequency Distributions

I. TERMS AND SYMBOLS TO REVIEW

Score	Width of interval (i)
Frequency (f)	Range (R)
Simple frequency distribution	Number of cases (N)
Grouped frequency distribution	Apparent limits
Class interval	Real limits
Class limits	Midpoint
	Stem and leaf display

II. SHORT-ANSWER QUESTIONS

In answering the questions in this section, base your answers on the frequency distribution shown below.

Class	f
30–32	1
27–29	2
24–26	5
21–23	3
18–20	1
--	2

1. The i for each interval is _____.

2. The limits of the lowest class have not been filled in. What are they? _____.

3. N is equal to what value? _____.

4. The values 30–32 in the topmost class interval represent the (a) _____ limits of the class. The (b) _____ limits of the class are (c) _____.

5. The midpoint of the class 24–26 is _____.

6. The approximate range (R) is _____. (Since the scores are grouped, the exact range cannot be determined.)

Answers

1. 3   2. 15–17   3. 14   4. (a) apparent   (b) real   (c) 29.5–32.5   5. 25
6. $32 - 15 = 17$

III.   FURTHER EXERCISES

1.   In a study of child-rearing practices, an investigator observed 50 kindergarten children and rated them on their liking for novel stimuli. He also obtained information about the children's treatment by their parents. The children were divided into two groups of 25. In one group were children whose parents actively encouraged them to do things on their own and make their own decisions; in the second group were children whose parents did not allow this kind of independence. The scores of the two groups are shown below, with high scores indicating a liking for novel stimuli.

(a)   Arrange the scores of the Encouraged group in a grouped frequency distribution, choosing a value for i that will best reveal the pattern of scores. For convenience, set the upper limit of the highest class interval at the value of the largest score in the distribution. Add up the frequency column to make sure that you have accounted for all 25 cases.

(b)   Using the same class intervals, arrange the scores of the Discouraged group into a frequency distribution.

(c)   Compare the two distributions. Does it appear that parental treatment had an effect on children's liking for novel stimuli?

(a)   Encouraged Group

48	51	51	Class	(Tallies)	f
52	42	45			
47	48	53			
49	50	38			
40	54	49			
59	45	31			
41	49	55			
45	44				
37	39				

(b)   Discouraged Group

42	36	37	Class	(Tallies)	f
37	53	41			
39	41	30			
31	38	51			
44	46	42			
36	26	34			
29	40	43			
40	27				
32	39				

19

(c)   Comparison of groups

2. Thirty high school seniors were given a 50-item quiz testing their knowledge of current events. Arrange their scores, shown below, in a stem and leaf display.

35	23	39
28	32	29
19	47	11
32	18	33
49	38	24
25	22	13
43	41	44
27	16	26
23	32	15
29	20	30

3. Several frequency distributions are reproduced below. For each distribution, indicate whether you consider the particular arrangement that has been chosen as the most *appropriate* way to handle the data or as *inappropriate*. If inappropriate, state why and what changes you would suggest.

(a)

Class	f
90–92	1
87–89	
84–86	1
81–83	
78–80	2
75–77	
72–74	1

(c)

Class	f
180–189	16
170–179	28
160–169	31
150–159	13

Answer: _____

Answer: _____

20

(b)

Class	f
24	1
23	0
22	1
21	1
20	2
19	2
18	3
17	2
16	0
15	3
14	0
13	2
12	1

Answer: _____

(d)

Class	f
16–17	2
14–15	4
12–13	8
10–11	9
8–9	5
6–7	3

Answer: _____

Section E

Problems for Chapter 3:
Graphic Representations

I. TERMS AND SYMBOLS TO REVIEW

Frequency polygon   Percentile rank
Horizontal (X) axis or abscissa   Quartile (Q)
Vertical (Y) axis or ordinate   Median (Mdn)
Cumulative frequency (cum f)   Deciles
Unimodal curve   Symmetrical distribution
Bimodal curve   Positive and negative skew
Cumulative frequency polygon   Bell-shaped distribution
Cumulative percentage   Line graph
Percentile   Bar graph
                                      Histogram

II. SHORT-ANSWER QUESTIONS

1. In a histogram graphing a frequency distribution, the Y axis is marked off to show

    (a) _____, and the X axis is marked off to show (b) _____

    (simple frequency distribution) or (c) _____ (grouped frequency

    distribution).

2. Frequency distributions are also graphed by means of a (a) _____ _____. In a histogram, frequencies are represented by (b) _____ and in a polygon, they are represented by (c) _____ plotted above each (d) _____ (simple frequency distribution) or (e) _____ (grouped frequency distribution).

3. In a histogram or frequency polygon, the length of the Y axis should be about _____% of the length of the X axis.

4. Another name for the cumulative polygon is _____.

5. In a cumulative polygon, the Y axis is marked off to show (a) _____ and the X axis is marked off to show (b) _____.

6. Cumulative frequencies can be translated into cumulative percents, thus yielding what is called a _____.

7. The percentile rank of a score is a value indicating (a) _____ _____. A percentile is the score (b) _____ _____.

8. The median is equal to the (a) _____ percentile, the (b) _____ quartile, or the (c) _____ decile.

9. A frequency polygon that has a single hump is called (a) _____ and one that has two humps is called (b) _____.

10. An asymmetrical, unimodal polygon in which the scores tail off at the upper end is called (a) _____. One in which the scores tail off at the lower end is called (b) _____.

11. The numbers of members in categorical groups or the average amount of some property exhibited by members of categorical groups are represented graphically by means of a _____.

12. In a bar graph, the bars _____ touch each other.

13. Changes in a performance measure that take place with systematic increases in the value of some variable are represented graphically by means of a (a) _____ in which values of the (b) _____ are represented on the Y axis and values of the (c) _____ are represented on the X axis.

Answers

1. (a) frequencies   (b) scores   (c) midpoints of class intervals   2. (a) frequency polygon
(b) bars   (c) points   (d) score   (e) midpoint of class interval   3. 75%   4. ogive
5. (a) cumulative frequencies (or percents)   (b) upper real limits of the scores or class intervals
6. percentile scale   7. (a) the percentage of the cases falling at or below the score   (b) at or
below which the specified percentage of the cases fall   8. (a) 50th   (b) 2nd   (c) 5th

9. (a) unimodal   (b) bimodal   10. (a) positively skewed   (b) negatively skewed
11. bar graph   12. should not (touch)   13. (a) line graph   (b) measure of performance
(c) variable

III.   MATCHING QUESTIONS

Several sets of data are described below. For each, choose the appropriate method of graphing the data.

　　　　(a) frequency polygon or histogram　　　(b) cumulative frequency polygon
　　　　(c) bar graph　　　　　　　　　　　　　(d) line graph

_____ 1. The maximum number of push-ups that each of 100 male freshmen is able to perform. The pattern of the group of scores is of interest.

_____ 2. The average number of children per family among five groups of different religious faiths.

_____ 3. An individual's average reaction time 15 minutes, 30 minutes, 45 minutes, and 60 minutes after drinking 2 oz of hard liquor.

_____ 4. The scores of medical school applicants on a medical aptitude test. Of interest is the performance of the applicants relative to each other.

_____ 5. The number of votes received by each of the 4 candidates in a city's last mayoral election.

Answers

1. (a)   2. (c)   3. (d)   4. (b)   5. (c)

IV. FURTHER EXERCISES

1. In the set of problems for the previous chapter, Problem III 2 presented the quiz scores for 30
    high school students and asked you to arrange the scores in a stem and leaf display. One such
    arrangement is shown in (a) below.

    (a) Plot the data in the form of a histogram, using the same class intervals as the stem and
        leaf display.

Stem	Leaf
4*	7 9
4	1 3 4
3*	5 8 9
3	0 2 2 2 3
2*	5 6 7 8 9 9
2	0 2 3 3 4
1*	5 6 8 9
1	1 3

    (b) Compare the two methods of graphing the data. What advantages does the stem and
    leaf display have over the histogram?

2. A group of military pilots and a group of male civilians of similar age and background are given a test measuring intensity of reaction to physical stress, with the results shown below. (Low scores indicate relatively low reactivity.)

Class	Military f	Civilian f
30–32		1
27–29	1	1
24–26	1	3
21–23	2	6
18–20	4	7
15–17	7	9
12–14	8	6
9–11	10	4
6–8	5	2
3–5	2	1

(a) Draw a single figure, showing the polygon for each of the two distributions. (Be sure to put the appropriate labels on the graph and give the graph a title.)

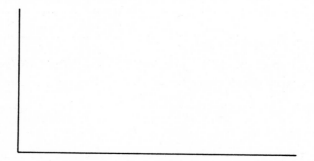

(b) Describe the shape of each distribution and compare the two groups.

28

3. Plot in a single graph cumulative frequency polygons for the distributions from the two groups in problem 2 above.

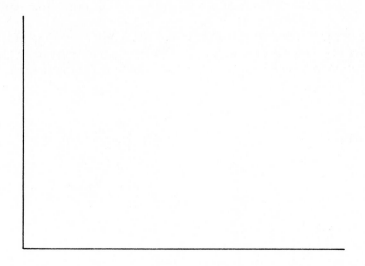

4. A test of verbal fluency was given to two groups of college students, one majoring in English and the other in engineering. The frequency distributions obtained from the two groups are plotted below in the form of cumulative percentage curves.

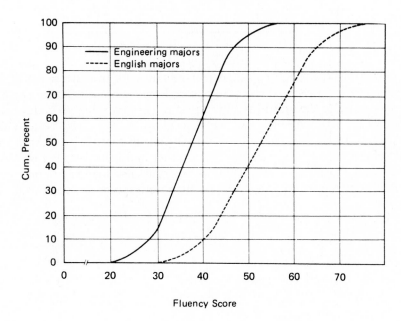

(a) The median for English majors is _____ and for engineering majors is _____.

(b) The first quartile for the English majors is _____.

(c) Kay C. Jones, an engineering major, earned a score of 45. Her percentile rank is

_____.

(d) The sixth decile for engineering majors is _____.

29

(e) The score of 60 has a percentile rank of _____ for English majors.

(f) Shelly Keats, an English major, scored 55. Had he been an engineering major, he would have had to obtain a score of only _____ to earn the same percentile rank.

5. Data have been collected on the average daily use of leisure time by adult men and women. The number of hours per day for four categories are reported below for the two sexes. Graph the information in a single figure in a form that will make the information stand our clearly.

	Men	Women
Television	1.8	1.4
Socializing	1.3	2.0
Reading	.8	.5
Other	1.5	1.5

6. An investigator studying memory asked college students to learn a list of 25 two-syllable words. The subjects read each word as it appeared on a screen and after seeing all 25 words, wrote down as many of the words as they could remember. This procedure was repeated 10 more times (trials), with the order in which the words appeared being changed on each occasion. For each of these trials, after the first presentation the experimenter divided the words each subject correctly recalled into those that had been recalled on the previous trial ("old" words) and those that had not ("new" words). The average number of new and old words recalled by the group of students was then determined for each trial, with the results that follow:

Trial	Old Words	New Words
1	3.4	5.9
2	5.8	5.4
3	7.5	5.3
4	8.8	5.4
5	11.1	5.2
6	10.1	5.2
7	10.7	5.3
8	11.6	5.1
9	12.5	5.0
10	13.3	4.9

30

(a) Graph the data in one figure.

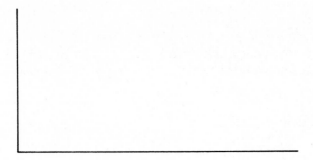

(b) Describe and compare the group's performance on the two types of items over the 10 trials.

Section F

Problems for Chapter 4:
Measures of
Central Tendency

I.   TERMS AND SYMBOLS TO REVIEW

Measure of central tendency Σ (sum of)
Arithmetic mean μ (mu)
$\bar{X}$ Deviation score (x)
Mode (Mo)   Percentile
Median (Mdn)   Percentile rank

II.   SHORT-ANSWER QUESTIONS

1. The sum of any set of quantities divided by the number of quantities is known as the

    _____ of the set of quantities.

2. The symbol $\bar{X}$ is a generalized expression for the mean of a _____

    _____.

3. The symbol μ is an expression for _____

    _____.

4. A very large number of samples are drawn from some population, $\bar{X}$ is found for each sample,

    and then the mean of the $\bar{X}$'s is calculated. The value of the mean of the $\bar{X}$'s takes the same

    value as the population _____.

5. Random sample $\bar{X}$'s show no systematic tendency to be (a) _____

_____ than the μ of the population from which they were drawn. The mean of a

random sample ($\bar{X}$) is (b) _____ estimate of the value of the

mean of the population (μ) from which it was drawn.

6. A deviation score is symbolized as (a) _____ and is obtained by (b) _____

_____.

7. The sum of the deviation scores from the mean of a distribution is symbolized as (a) _____

and is always equal to (b) _____.

8. In a simple frequency distribution, the mode is that score that (a) _____

_____

and in a grouped frequency distribution, the mode is (b) _____

_____.

9. The median is that score (a) _____

_____.

The median can also be defined as (b) _____ in an ordered group of

scores.

10. Of the three measures of central tendency, which measure is affected by the exact value of

every score? (a) _____. Which measure is most stable from sample to sample?

(b) _____.

11. In a symmetrical, unimodal distribution, the values of the mean, median, and mode are

_____.

12. Starting from the peak and going toward the tail of a skewed unimodal distribution, the

order of the three measures of central tendency is _____.

13. The reason that the mean is nearer the tail in skewed distributions than the mode and the

median is that _____.

14. The quantity $\Sigma Y/N$ is the _____ of the Y scores.

Answers

1. mean   2. sample   3. the mean of a population   4. μ (mu)   5. (a) either larger or
smaller   (b) an unbiased estimate   6. (a) x (b) subtracting $\bar{X}$ from X   7. (a) Σx (b) 0
8. (a) occurs most frequently   (b) the midpoint of the interval with the highest frequency
9. (a) at or below which 50% of the cases fall   (b) the middle score   10. (a) mean   (b) mean
11. the same   12. mode, median, mean   13. the exact value of every score determines the
mean so that it is more sensitive to extreme scores in a distribution   14. mean or $\bar{Y}$

III. MULTIPLE-CHOICE QUESTIONS

Put your answer in the blank at the left.

_____ 1. The mean and mode of a unimodal distribution are both 42. The most likely value of the median is: (a) 42   (b) greater than 42   (c) less than 42   (d) can't tell from the information given.

_____ 2. The median of a unimodal distribution is 30 and the mode is 35. The value of the mean is most likely: (a) greater than 35   (b) less than 30   (c) some value between 30 and 35   (d) can't tell from the information given.

_____ 3. The mean of a unimodal distribution was calculated and found to take the same value as the 55th percentile. The distribution was: (a) symmetrical (b) negatively skewed   (c) positively skewed   (d) can't tell   (e) the calculations had to have been in error.

_____ 4. The expression Σx is equal to: (a) $\Sigma X - \Sigma \bar{X}$ (b) $\Sigma X - N\bar{X}$ (c) 0   (d) $\Sigma(X - \bar{X})$ (e) all of the above.

_____ 5. The mean of a random sample from a given population is 84. The best estimate of the population mean is: (a) 84   (b) greater than 84   (c) less than 84   (d) there's no way of making a good estimate.

_____ 6. In a symmetrical bell-shaped distribution, the median is 103 and the 40th percentile is 90. The value of the 60th percentile is: (a) greater than 103   (b) 116   (c) the same as the 6th decile   (d) all of the above   (e) none of the above.

_____ 7. The measure of central tendency that best represents the typical case in a skewed distribution is the: (a) mean   (b) median   (c) mode   (d) all three are equally representative.

_____ 8. An instructor decides to give half the class A's and B's and the other half C's and below as exam grades. The exam score dividing the B's and C's is: (a) the mean (b) median   (c) mode   (d) dependent on the shape of the distribution.

_____ 9. In a sample of 50 cases, the median, defined as the middle case, is obtained. Then the median, defined as the point at or below which 50% of the cases fall, is calculated from the simple frequency distribution of the scores. The value(s) of the two medians: (a) are identical   (b) are close but not necessarily identical (c) are likely to be quite different, especially if the distribution is skewed   (d) is likely to be higher for the middle case   (e) is likely to be lower for the middle case.

Answers

1. (a)   2. (b)   3. (c)   4. (e)   5. (a)   6. (d)   7. (c)   8. (b)   9. (b)

IV. CALCULATIONAL PROBLEMS

In the problems below, you are asked to determine a measure of central tendency or a percentile rank or percentile. Several examples of each type of problem are included. If you have difficulty solving a particular type of problem, try another for additional practice. If you have no difficulty in finding the correct answer, you might go on to the next type of problem. You are reminded that the list of formulas in Appendix II of the text and the summary of useful formulas printed on the endpapers of the text are reproduced at the back of the *Workbook*. You should find it convenient to use these lists in computing the statistics called for in this section and in later chapters. Consult the text for explanations of the formulas or the Step by Step Procedures section of each chapter for illustrations of their use.

A tip is in order. Before you attempt your calculations, it is always wise to "eyeball" the data and estimate the answer, and then to check the result of your calculations with your estimate. If they are grossly different, go back and check your work. Did you use the correct formula? Did you enter the right values into the formula? Did you make an arithmetic error?

1. For each of the following sets of numbers, find the mean and the median. (Use the middle case method for determining the median.)

   (a) 3, 10, 2, 5

   $\bar{X}$ _____   Mdn _____

   (b) 7, 5, 13, 9

   $\bar{X}$ _____   Mdn _____

   (c) 6, 11, 15, 20

   $\bar{X}$ _____   Mdn _____

2. For each of the following simple frequency distributions, find the mean and mode.

   (a)

Score	f
10	2
9	1
8	4
7	2
6	1

   $\bar{X}$ _____   Mode _____

   (b)

Score	f
12	1
11	1
10	0
9	6
8	4
7	1

   $\bar{X}$ _____   Mode _____

3. For each of the following grouped frequency distributions, find the mean, approximate median, and mode.

(a)

Class	f
16–18	2
13–15	4
10–12	5
7–9	1
4–6	1
1–3	2

Mean _____   Median _____   Mode _____

(b)

Class	f
30–34	1
25–29	3
20–24	4
15–19	2
10–14	2

Mean _____   Median _____   Mode _____

4. For the grouped frequency distribution shown below, approximate the value of the third quartile (Q_3), second decile, and 35th percentile.

Class	f
32–34	2
29–31	3
26–28	3
23–25	4
20–22	5
17–19	7
14–16	6
11–13	4
8–10	3
5–7	3
	$\Sigma f = 40$

Q_3 = _____

2nd decile = _____

35th percentile = _____

Answers

1. (a) $\bar{X} = 20/4 = 5$ Mdn = 4
   (b) $\bar{X} = 34/4 = 8.5$ Mdn = 8
   (c) $\bar{X} = 52/4 = 13$ Mdn = 13

2. (a) $\bar{X} = \Sigma fX/N = 81/10 = 8.1$ Mo = 8
   (b) $\bar{X} = 116/13 = 8.9$ Mo = 9

3. (a) $\bar{X} = 162/15 = 10.8$ Mo = 11   Mdn = 11
   (b) $\bar{X} = 259/12 = 21.58$ Mo = 22   Mdn = 22

4. $Q_3 = 24$ (75% of N = 30; 30th case = 24)   2nd decile = 12 (8th case)   (35th percentile = 15 (14th case)

38

V. FURTHER EXERCISES

Items 1–6 present a pair of similar expressions. For each member of the pair, describe how the quantity called for in the expression should be obtained. Be sure your statements are precise enough to indicate the *differences* in the operations used in the two expressions.

Illustrate your understanding of each expression by finding its value, based on the data shown. (The data show five pairs of scores, one for Y and one for X; the XY column shows the product of each pair of scores). Put the value of each expression in the box at the right of the item.

X	Y	XY
6	8	48
2	5	10
4	7	28
5	6	30
3	4	12

1. (a) ΣX^2

   (b) $(\Sigma X)^2$

2. (a) $(\Sigma X)(\Sigma Y)$ where there is a pair of scores, X and Y, for each of the N cases

   (b) ΣXY

3. (a) $\Sigma(X - \bar{X})$

   (b) $\Sigma X - \bar{X}$

4. (a) $\Sigma X^2/N$

   (b) $(\Sigma X/N)^2$

5. (a) $\Sigma(X - \bar{X})^2$

(b) $\Sigma X - \bar{X}^2$

6. (a) $\Sigma(XY)/N$

(b) $(\Sigma X/N)(\Sigma Y/N)$

7. Shown below is a bell-shaped, symmetrical polygon. The median of the distribution has been calculated to be 32 and the 60th percentile to be 34. Indicate on the baseline your guess about the position of the percentiles listed below. (Hint: Think about the relationship among percent of cases, N, and percent of area under the curve.)

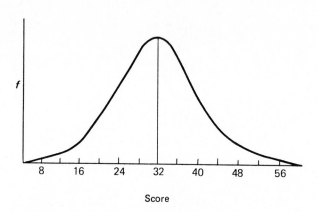

Score

Percentiles: (a) 40th   (b) 70th   (c) 90th   (d) 20th
(e) explain the rationale of your choices

8. On a statistics examination, students were given the frequency distributions shown below and for each, asked to compute the mean. The answers of one student are shown at the right of each distribution. Determine *by inspection* (not by calculation) whether the answers appear to be *reasonable* or *unreasonable*. (E.g., if the scores range from 0 to 40 and $\bar{X}$ was stated to be 41, the answer is obviously unreasonable.) If the value seems reasonable for the mean, write R in the answer blank; if the value seems unreasonable, write your estimate of the correct value in the answer blank. Justify your choice of these values at the right of the distribution.

(a)

Distribution		Student's Answer	Answer
Class	f		
97–99	1		
94–96	3		
91–93	4	$\bar{X} = 82.72$	_____
88–90	5		
85–87	5		
82–84	8		
79–81	13		
76–78	9		
73–75	6		
	$\Sigma f = 54$		

(b)

Distribution		Student's Answer	Answer
Class	f		
70–74	2		
65–69	1		
60–64	4	$\bar{X} = 50.28$	_____
55–59	6		
50–54	10		
45–49	5		
40–44	3		
35–39	2		
30–34	2		
	$\Sigma f = 35$		

(c)

Distribution		Student's Answer	Answer
Class	f		
21–22	3		
19–20	5		
17–18	9	$\bar{X} = 18.34$	_____
15–16	6		
13–14	4		
11–12	2		
9–10	3		
7–8	1		
5–6	2		
3–4	1		
	$\Sigma f = 36$		

41

9. Suppose that the following symmetrical distribution has been obtained and $\overline{X}$, Mdn, and Mo computed. Suppose further that it is later discovered that several scores were incorrectly recorded. The items below indicate several sets of such scores and their correct values. If the three measures of central tendency were recomputed with the correct scores, indicate at the right what would happen to the value of each shift upward (U), shift downward (D), or no change (No).

Class	f
71–73	1
68–70	3
65–67	4
62–64	6
59–61	8
56–58	10
53–55	8
50–52	6
47–49	4
44–46	3
41–43	1
	$\Sigma f = 55$

(a)

Original Scores	Corrected Scores	Direction of Change
44	47	(U, D, No)
50	51	$\overline{X}$ _____
64	67	Mdn _____
		Mo _____

(b)

Original Scores	Corrected Scores	Direction of Change
53	59	(U, D, No)
47	64	$\overline{X}$ _____
		Mdn _____
		Mo _____

(c)

Original Scores	Corrected Scores	Direction of Change
68	65	(U, D, No)
50	49	$\overline{X}$ _____
44	47	Mdn _____
64	65	Mo _____

10. State the conditions under which changes in score values will or will not affect the value of each measure of central tendency.

11. In some of the following situations you will find that one or more of the measures of central tendency are impossible to compute from the data available. In other cases, all of them can be computed but one measure is most appropriate. For each of the situations of the first type, indicate which measures of central tendency would be impossible to compute and why. For the second type, indicate the most appropriate measure and the reason for your choice.

(a) A poll was taken in which a group of successful business executives reported how many hours a week, on the average, they devoted to work. The following results were reported:

Hours	f
51 or more	25
46–50	12
41–45	8
36–40	6
31–35	4

(b) An extremely difficult 50-point examination was given in which most of the students clustered around 10–15, although there was a scattering of students who earned better scores, all the way up to the upper 40s. If a measure representative of the typical student were required, what measure should be used?

43

(c)   Prior to conducting further statistical analyses, an experimenter examines the frequency polygons of the two groups he has tested and finds both of them to be nearly symmetrical bell-shaped distributions.

(d)   In an investigation of the process of concept identification, 35 subjects were given repeated trials until they correctly identified the concepts. If they did not succeed in 20 trials, however, trials were terminated. "Scores" were the number of trials to mastery. The three subjects who did not solve the tasks in 20 trials were given scores of 20+.

Section G

Problems for Chapter 5:
Variability

I. TERMS AND SYMBOLS TO REVIEW

Semi-interquartile range σ and σ^2
Average deviation s and s^2
Variance   Point estimation
Standard deviation   Degrees of freedom (df)
S and S^2 z score

II. SHORT-ANSWER QUESTIONS

1. The scores obtained by two groups on the same measure are plotted below. In what two major ways do the groups differ?_____

_____.

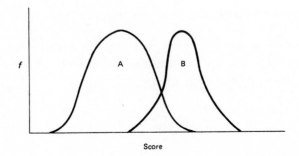

2. The range, semi-interquartile range, average deviation, variance, and standard deviation are all measures of (a) _____. Of these, the least satisfactory measure is the (b) _____. The measures whose values are determined by the exact value of every score in the distribution are the (c) _____

_____.

3. Half the score distance between Q_1 and Q_3 is called the _____

_____.

4. The quantity $\Sigma x / N$ represents (a) _____. It is never used as a measure of variability because (b) _____.

5. The quantity $\Sigma |x| / N$ is called the (a) _____ and is obtained by (b) _____.
It is less preferable as a measure of variability than the variance and the standard deviation because (c) _____

_____.

6. The variance is the mean of (a) _____ and is obtained by (b) _____. The standard deviation is obtained by (c) _____.

7. The symbol used to identify the variance of a *sample* is (a) _____. The symbol used to identify the variance of a *population* is (b) _____. The corresponding symbols for the standard deviations are (c) _____.

8. The variances of samples drawn from some population tend to be (a) _____ in size than the population variance and thus are (b) _____ estimates of the population value.

9. The symbol (a) _____indicates an unbiased estimate of the population variance based on sample data. It is obtained by reducing (b) _____ by (c) _____ in the (d) _____ of the equation for S^2.

10. The corrected estimate of the population standard deviation based on sample data is symbolized as (a) _____and is found by (b) _____

_____.

11. The procedure of estimating the precise value of a population parameter from sample data is known as making a _____.

12. The number of values that are free to vary in a distribution, once certain requirements are met, is known as _____.

13. In the series of N quantities that must sum to a specified value, *df* is equal to (a) _____, which is also the denominator in the formula for s^2. The formula for s^2 can thus be rewritten to read (b) _____.

14. The formulas defining the variance and standard deviation employ deviation (x) scores. For calculational purposes it is more convenient to rearrange these formulas into a form that employs only _____.

15. A z score is a (a) _____ expressed in (b) _____ units. Thus, a z of +1.00 represents a score that falls (c) _____ unit (d) _____ the mean and a z of –2.50 represents a score that falls (e) _____.

16. Scores can be translated back and forth between the raw score scale and the z score scale. In a distribution with a mean of 36 and a standard deviation of 3, the raw score equivalent of $z = -2.33$ is _____.

17. In a set of z scores, the mean always has the value (a) _____ and the variance and standard deviation always have the value (b) _____.

18. A z score is also known as a _____.

19. Standard scores obtained by multiplying each z score by 10 and adding 50 to the product are known as (a) _____. In this system, a z of +1.50 would be equal to a score of (b) _____.

20. In a system of standard scores in which each z score is multiplied by 100 and 500 is added to the product, the mean of the standard scores is (a) _____ and the standard deviation is (b) _____.

21. In a large bell-shaped distribution, R was 39. You estimate s to be _____.

Answers

1. Group A is more variable (heterogeneous, dispersed) and the mean of Group A is smaller than that of Group B   2. (a) variability   (b) range   (c) variance and standard deviation
3. semi-interquartile range   4. (a) the mean of the deviations of the scores from the mean of the distribution   (b) it always equals 0   5. (a) average deviation   (b) finding the mean of the absolute deviations from the mean   (c) it ignores signs of x's (is based on absolute deviations) and thus is nonalgebraic   6. (a) the squared deviations from the mean   (b) squaring each deviation, summing, and dividing by N   (c) extracting the square root of the variance
7. (a) S^2 (b) σ^2 (c) S and σ 8. (a) smaller   (b) biased   9. (a) s^2 (b) N   (c) 1   (d) denominator   10. (a) s (b) extracting the square root of s^2 11. point estimation
12. degrees of freedom (df)   13. (a) N – 1   (b) $\Sigma x^2/df$ 14. raw scores   15. (a) raw score   (b) standard deviation units   (c) one standard deviation   (d) above   (e) $2\,^1\!/_2$ standard deviation units below the mean   16. 29   17. (a) 0   (b) 1   18. standard score
19. (a) T scores   (b) 65   20. (a) 500   (b) 100   21. 1/6 (R) = 39/6 = 6.5

III. MULTIPLE-CHOICE QUESTIONS

Put your answer in the blank at the left.

_____ 1. The range and s for each of a series of distributions are reported below. Which set of scores is the most variable? (a) $R = 15, s = 2$ (b) $R = 25, s = 4$ (c) $R = 20, s = 3$ (d) $R = 25, s = 5$ (e) both (b) and (d).

_____ 2. The 25th percentile is 22 and the 75th percentile is 36. The semi-interquartile range is: (a) 14 (b) 7 (c) 1 (d) can't tell without knowing N.

_____ 3. The value of the average deviation is closest to the value of the: (a) range (b) semi-interquartile range (c) variance (d) standard deviation.

_____ 4. The S of a sample has been calculated as 3.5. The best estimate of the σ of the population from which the sample was drawn is: (a) 3.5 (b) greater than 3.5 (c) less than 3.5 (d) no way to estimate with information given.

_____ 5. As sample N's increase, the degree to which S^2 tends to underestimate σ^2: (a) decreases (b) increases (c) stays the same.

_____ 6. In a sample of 500 cases whose distribution is bell-shaped the range is 36. The S of the distribution can be estimated to be approximately: (a) 6 (b) 12 (c) 18 (d) 24 (e) no way to estimate from information given.

_____ 7. The quantity s: (a) is a slightly biased estimate of σ (b) is a corrected estimate of σ (c) is an unbiased estimate of σ (d) both (a) and (b) (e) both (b) and (c).

_____ 8. In the set of numbers, 3, 4, 7, 9, 12, df is equal to: (a) 5 (b) 4 (c) 3 (d) 2 (e) 1.

_____ 9. In two groups of 50 cases each, the mean and standard deviation are, respectively, 83 and 6 for Group 1, and 75 and 5 for Group 2. The mean and standard deviation of the z scores in each group are: (a) equal in the two groups (b) greater in Group 1 (c) greater in Group 2 (d) insufficient information to tell.

_____ 10. A set of standard scores has been developed to produce a mean of 100 and a standard deviation of 20. In the original raw score distribution, the mean was 62, and the standard deviation was 4. A raw score of 60 has a standard score equivalent of: (a) 80 (b) 90 (c) 100 (d) 110 (e) 120.

Answers

1. (d)   2. (b)   3. (d)   4. (b)   5. (a)   6. (a)   7. (d)   8. (b)   9. (a)
10. (b)

IV. CALCULATIONAL PROBLEMS

1. For each of the following ungrouped distributions, calculate S twice, once by the deviation method (Formula 5.3) and once by the raw score method (Formula 5.7 or 5.8).

48

(a)

Score
9
8
8
7
7
5
5
5
4
2

Deviation _____

Raw score _____

(b)

Score
31
26
21
14
13

Deviation _____

Raw score _____

2. For each of the distributions in problem 1, compute s twice, first using the deviation score formula (Formula 5.5) and then using the raw score formula (Formula 5.9). Note that you have already obtained or are given all the quantities entering into these formulas.

      (a) Deviation formula: _____

           Raw score formula: _____

      (b) Deviation formula: _____

           Raw score formula: _____

3. For each of the following frequency distributions, calculate s by the raw score method.

49

(a)

Class	f
14–16	2
11–13	3
8–10	5
5–7	3
2–4	2

Answer _____

(b)

Class	f
9	1
8	2
7	5
6	4
5	4
4	3
3	1

Answer _____

4. The μ and σ for several distributions are given below. Find the z score equivalents of the given raw scores and the raw score equivalents of the given z scores.

(a) $\mu = 119$ $\sigma = 10$

   $X = 125$ z = _____

   $X = 102$ z = _____

   $z = 2.50$ X = _____

   $z = -3.00$ X = _____

(b) $\mu = 73$ $\sigma = 8$

   $X = 79$ z = _____

   $X = 63$ z = _____

   $z = 2.25$ X = _____

   $z = -1.75$ X = _____

5. In each of the following, determine the standard score as described.

   (a) A distribution of raw scores has a mean of 61 and a standard deviation of 10. Using the formula, Standard score = 200(z) + 1000, determine the standard score of each of the following raw scores.

$$X = 71$$ Answers _____

$$X = 55$$ _____

$$X = 46$$ _____

   (b) A distribution has a mean of 82 and a standard deviation of 5. What are the T score equivalents of the following raw scores?

$$X = 77$$ Answers _____

$$X = 94$$ _____

$$X = 60$$ _____

Answers

1. (a) $\bar{X} = 60/10 = 6$. Deviation method: Subtract $\bar{X}$ from each X to find x; square each x and sum the x^2's; $S = \sqrt{\Sigma x^2/N} = \sqrt{42/10} = 2.05$. Raw score method: Square each X and sum the squares; $S = \sqrt{\Sigma X^2/N - \bar{X}^2} = \sqrt{402/10 - (6^2)} = 2.05$.   (b) $\bar{X} = 105/5 = 21$. Deviation method: $S = \sqrt{238/5} = 6.90$. Raw score method: $S = \sqrt{2443/5 - (21)^2} = \sqrt{47.6} = 6.90$.

2. (a) Deviation: $s = \sqrt{42/(10-1)} = 2.16$. Raw score: $s = \sqrt{[402 - (60)^2/10]/(10-1)} = \sqrt{4.667} = 2.16$.
(b) Deviation: $s = \sqrt{238/4} = 7.71$. Raw score: $s = \sqrt{[2443 - (105)^2/5]/(5-1)} = \sqrt{59.5} = 7.71$.

3. (a) Find midpoint (X) of each interval and then fX and fX^2. The sums of the fX and fX^2 columns are equal to 135 and 1413. By Formula 5.10, $s = \sqrt{[1413 - (135)^2/15]/(15-1)} = \sqrt{198/14} = 3.76$.   (b) $s = \sqrt{[755 - (119)^2/20]/(20-1)} = \sqrt{46.95/19} = 1.57$.

4. $z = (X - \mu)/\sigma; X = \mu + (\sigma)(z)$.   (a) $z = (125 - 119)/10 = .6; z = (102 - 119)/10 = -1.7; X = 119 + (10) (2.5) = 144; X = 119 + (10) (-3) = 89$.   (b) $z = (79 - 73)/8 = .75; z = (63 - 73)/8 = -1.25; X = 73 + (8) (2.25) = 91; X = 73 + (8) (-1.75) = 59$.

5. Standard score = 200 (z) + 1000.   (a) SS = 200 [(71 - 61)/10] + 1000 = 1200; SS = 200 [(55 - 61)/10] + 1000 = -120 + 1000 = 880; SS = 200 (-1.5) + 1000 = 700.   (b) T score = 10 (z) + 50; T = 10(-1.00) + 50 = 40; T = 10 (2.4) + 50 = 74; T = 10 (-4.4) + 50 = 6.

V. FURTHER EXERCISES

1. In the following problems, two sets of scores are implied. For each problem, indicate which set you think will show the greater variability and why.

    (a) The heights of members of the Notre Dame football team versus the heights of all men enrolled in that university.

    (b) Scores on the Quantitative section of the Graduate Record Examination for students applying to graduate school in psychology and in mathematics.

    (c) The average yearly rainfall over the past 20 years for Chicago, Illinois, and the Sahara Desert.

    (d) The bowling scores made by a talented individual just taking up the game versus a bowling professional.

2. The number of movies attended last month by a group of first-year law school students is shown below:

X	f	
6	1	_____
5	0	_____
4	2	_____
3	3	_____
2	3	_____
1	4	_____

(a) Compute the variance of the distribution by the deviation method.

Answer _____

(b) Compute the variance by the raw score method.

Answer _____

3. (a) A frequency polygon is shown below that has a mean of 80 and a standard deviation (s) of 10. Suppose that 40 is added to every score in the distribution on which the polygon is based. Draw a polygon for this new distribution on the same graph as the original, and indicate the value of $\overline{X}$ and s.

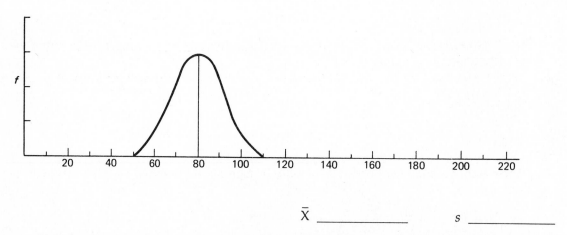

$\overline{X}$ _____   s _____

(b) The same polygon as in (a) is reproduced on the next page. Now suppose that each score had instead been multiplied by 2. Draw the polygon for this new distribution and indicate the value of $\overline{X}$ and s.

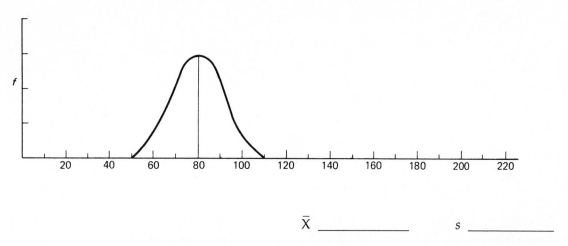

$\overline{X}$ _____ s _____

(c) Suppose that 50 was subtracted from every score. Draw the new polygon and indicate the value of $\overline{X}$ and s.

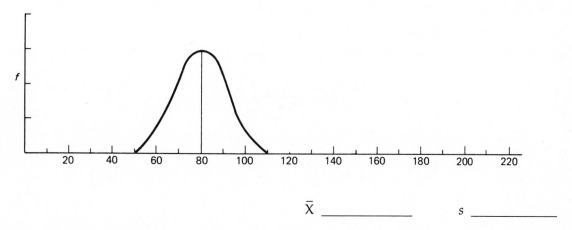

$\overline{X}$ _____ s _____

(d) Draw the polygon that would result if each score had 40 subtracted from it and as then divided by 2. Indicate the $\overline{X}$ and s.

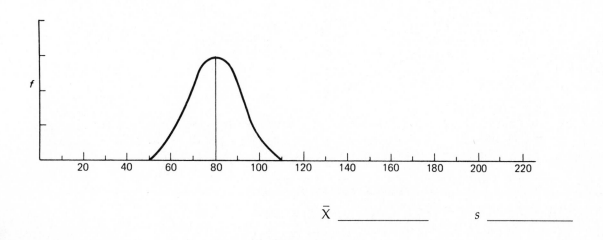

$\overline{X}$ _____ s _____

55

(e) Make a general statement about what happens to the mean and to the standard deviation when scores in a distribution (1) have a constant added or subtracted, and (2) are multiplied or divided by a constant.

4. Summary statistics for all 500 members of a population are shown below. Also shown is the frequency distribution for a sample drawn at random from the population.

Population Data

Range:	1–17
ΣX:	4500
ΣX^2:	43,380
N:	500

Sample

X	f
17	1
16	
15	
14	1
13	
12	2
11	4
10	9
9	13
8	8
7	5
6	4
5	1
4	1
3	1

$\Sigma f = 90$

$\Sigma f X = 441$

$\Sigma f X^2 = 4161$

(a) Find μ, σ^2, and σ.

μ _____

σ^2 _____

σ _____

(b) If you had only the sample data, what would you guess as the most likely value of μ? Does your estimated value of μ coincide with the value found in (a)? If not, why?

(c) Compute S^2 and s^2 for the sample data. Which is closer to σ^2? Why?

S^2 _____

s^2 _____

5. For each of the following distributions, *estimate* (but do not compute) the standard deviation, based on the relationship between the standard deviation and R.

(a)

X	f
90	2
89	4
88	6
87	9
86	10
85	12
84	16
83	11
82	10
81	8
80	7
79	3
78	2
	$\Sigma f = 100$

Answer: _____

(b)

Class	f
150–154	1
145–149	3
140–144	6
135–139	10
130–134	16
125–129	19
120–124	25
115–119	29
110–114	26
105–109	18
100–104	15
95–99	12
90–94	6
85–89	2
80–84	2
	$\Sigma f = 190$

Answer: _____

6. Data have been collected nationally from 10,000 fifth graders on a test of reading comprehension and a test of arithmetic skills.

Reading	Arithmetic
$\mu = 104$	$\mu = 64$
$\sigma = 10$	$\sigma = 8$

$$z = \frac{X - M}{\sigma}$$

(a) The scores of 3 children in the fifth grade of the Grundy Center Elementary School are listed below. Find their z score on each test.

Pupil	Reading	Arithmetic	z_R	z_A
1	116	72	1.2	1
2	81	58	-2.3	.75
3	98	76	-.6	1.5

58

(b) Which child was most consistent in performance, in terms of relative standing, on the two tests? Which was least consistent?

Most _____1_____

Least _____2_____

(c) The z scores for three of the children are listed below. What are their raw scores?

Pupil	Reading z Score	Arithmetic z Score	Reading Raw Score	Arithmetic Raw Score
1	+1.40	+1.75	_____	_____
2	−2.60	−1.25	_____	_____
3	− .30	+2.50	_____	_____

(d) If one of the children had a 109 on the reading comprehension test, what *raw score* would he have had to make on the arithmetic skills test to earn the same z score on both tests?

Answer _____

Section H

Problems for Chapter 6:
Probability

I.   TERMS AND SYMBOLS TO REVIEW

Set	Independent events
Element	Nonindependent events
Mutually exclusive events	Conditional probability [$p(A \mid B)$]
Sampling with replacement	Joint events
Sampling without replacement	Permutation (P_N, P_r^N)
A and complement of A ($\bar{A}$)	Combination (C_r^N)
Addition rule [$p(A$ or $B)$]	N factorial (N!)63

Multiplication rule [$p(A, B)$]

II.   SHORT-ANSWER QUESTIONS

1.   Each object or event in a group is called an (a) _____ in a (b) _____ of objects or events. If, on any occasion, only one event can occur, the set of events is (c) _____ ; if more than one event can occur, the set of events is (d) _____ .

2.   An instructor's grading policy is to give half the class A's and B's and the other half C's or below. Getting A or B versus getting C or below are examples of events that are

(a) _____ likely. Some students enroll on a pass-fail basis (that is, if their grade is C or more, it is reported as pass). Pass and fail are examples of events that are

(b) _____ likely.

All the following questions assume a set of *mutually exclusive* events in which each element is *equally likely* unless otherwise specified.

3. In a set of 5 events, the probability of any one of the events occurring on a single occasion is

   (a) _____. In general, the probability of occurrence of any subset of events from a set of events is the ratio of (b) _____

   _____.

4. All the elements in a set that are *not* A are known as the (a) _____

   _____ symbolized as (b) _____.

5. In a group of 100 individuals, 50 are currently married, 25 have never been married, 20 are divorced, and 5 are widowed. The probability that a person is divorced or widowed is

   (a) _____. This probability was determined by using the (b) _____

   _____ rule.

6. The probability of each event occurring in a set of 10 is 1/10. The probability of the same event occurring twice in a row is (a) _____. This probability was determined by applying the (b) _____ rule.

7. In a set of 10 objects, A–J, one is to be selected at random and then another from the remaining 9. The probability of selecting object G and then object B is (a) _____.

   This probability was determined by applying the (b) _____ rule to

   (c) _____ probabilities for (d) _____

   events.

8. Employees are classified as having managerial or nonmanagerial positions and as being largely satisfied or dissatisfied with their job, thus yielding (a) _____ categories of individuals. This is an example of (b) _____ events. A table in which the proportion of the total group in each of the categories is shown is known as a

   (c) _____ table. Given the fact that an employee is a manager, what is the probability that the employee is dissatisfied? This questions inquires about a

   (d) _____ probability for (e) _____ events.

9. The product of the integers from N to 1 [N (N − 1) (N − 2) $\cdots$ 1] is called (a) _____

   _____ and is symbolized as (b) _____.

10. The number of different sequences that a set of objects can take is known as the number of

    (a) _____ and is equal to (b) _____.

11. When the number of possible permutations for N objects taken *r* at a time is to be determined, the number is determined by the formula _____.

12. Combinations differ from permutations of N objects taken *r* at a time in that they refer to the possible number of different subsets of objects (a) _____.

With N and *r* held constant, the number of combinations is (b) _____ than the number of permutations.

Answers

1. (a) element   (b) set   (c) mutually exclusive   (d) nonmutually exclusive   2. (a) equally
(b) not equally   3. (a) 1/5   (b) of the number of events belonging to the subset of events to the
total number of events   4. (a) complement of A   (b) $\bar{A}$ 5. (a) (20 + 5)/100 = .25
(b) addition   6. (a) (1/10) (1/10) = 1/100   (b) multiplication rule   7. (a) (1/10) (1/9) =
1/90   (b) multiplication   (c) conditional   (d) nonindependent   8. (a) 4   (b) joint
(c) probability   (d) conditional   (e) dependent   9. (a) N factorial   (b) N!
10. (a) permutations   (b) N!   11. $P_r^N = N!/(N-r)!$ 12. (a) without regard to sequence
(b) less

III. CALCULATIONAL PROBLEMS

1. A jar contains 20 balls, 4 yellow, 5 white, 8 blue, and 3 red. Determine the probability of drawing the following. (Leave your answers in fractional form.)

Answer

(a) On a single draw, yellow   _____

(b) On a single draw, not yellow   _____

(c) On a single draw, red or blue   _____

(d) On a single draw, blue or white   _____

(e) Drawing red and then, after replacing it, yellow   _____

(f) Drawing blue, followed by white, and then red (with replacement)   _____

(g) Drawing a white ball, followed by blue (without replacement)   _____

(h) Drawing a sequence of yellow, red, and red without replacement   _____

2. The 50 men in an experiment were given a problem-solving task that was rigged so that half solved it and half did not. They then were asked whether their performance was a reflection mostly of their own ability (or a lack of it), the difficulty level of the task, or how hard they tried (effort). The table below shows the number in the two experimental groups who made each choice.

	Ability	Effort	Difficulty	Total
Succeed	18	5	2	25
Fail	5	14	6	25
Total	23	19	8	50

(a) Set up a table (like Table 6.2 in the text) showing the proportion of the 50 individuals in each category.

(b)   Set up a table showing the conditional probability of an individual giving each explanation, given their experimental condition (see Table 6.3 in text).

(c)   Given that a person has succeeded, what is the probability that he chose ability as the reason for his success?

Answer _____

(d)   Given that a person has failed, what is the probability that he chose the difficulty of the task as the reason for his failure?

Answer _____

   Calculational tip: In the problems below calling for the division of one factorial by another, considerable labor can be saved by first canceling terms in the numerator and denominator.

Example:

$$\frac{5!}{3!} = \frac{(5)\ (4)\ (3)\ (2)\ (1)}{(3)\ (2)\ (1)} = (5)\ (4)$$

$$\frac{6!}{2!4!} = \frac{(6)\ (5)\ (4)\ (3)\ (2)\ (1)}{(2)\ (1)\ (4)\ (3)\ (2)\ (1)} = \frac{(6)\ (5)}{(2)\ (1)} = \frac{(3)\ (5)}{(1)}$$

64

3. In a set of 6 objects:

   (a) How many permutations of the 6 objects are there?

   Answer _____

   (b) How many permutations are there of the 6 objects taken 2 at a time?

   Answer _____

   (c) How many combinations are there of the 6 objects taken 2 at a time?

   Answer _____

4. In a set of 8 objects:

   (a) How many permutations are there of the objects taken 4 at a time?

   Answer _____

   (b) How many combinations are there of the objects taken 3 at a time?

   Answer _____

Answers

1. (a) 4/20 or 1/5   (b) 16/20 or 4/5   (c) 11/20   (d) 13/20   (e) (3/20) (4/20) = 3/100
(f) (8/20) (5/20) (3/20) = 3/200   (g) (5/20 (8/19) = 2/19   (h) (4/20) (3/19) (2/18) = 24/6840 =
1/285

2. (a)

	Ability	Effort	Difficulty	Total
Succeed	.36	.10	.04	.50
Fail	.10	.28	.12	.50
Total	.46	.38	.16	1.00

(b)

	Ability	Effort	Difficulty	Total
Succeed	.72	.20	.08	1.00
Fail	.20	.56	.24	1.00

(c) .72   (d) .24

3. (a) 720   (b) 6!/4! = 30   (c) 6!/(2!) (4!) = 15   4. (a) 8!/4! = 1680   (b) 8!/(3!) (5!) = 56

IV. FURTHER EXERCISES

1. A recently married couple plans to have three children. Assume that for each pregnancy, the probability of a multiple birth for this couple is 0 and that their probability of having a boy or a girl is .50-.50 (or 1/2-1/2).

   (a) The ideal outcome, the couple decides, is to have a boy followed by two girls. What is the probability that their preferred order will occur?

   Answer _____

   (b) What is the probability that with three children, all would be the same sex?

   Answer _____

   (c) Suppose that they were to have four children instead of three. What is the probability that the first three would be boys and the last a girl?

   Answer _____

   (d) What is the probability that of four children, two would be boys and two would be girls?

   Answer _____

   (e) Suppose that the couple had three boys and decide to try again for a girl, reasoning that the probability of a girl is now very much in their favor. How much in their favor?

   Answer _____

2. Bobby's mother has bought 10 toys to be given out as favors at his birthday party: 5 rubber balls, 3 puzzles, and 2 miniature cars. The favors are passed out at random to the guests.

(a) What is the probability that the first child to be given a toy received a ball?

Answer _____

(b) Given that the first child received a ball, what is the probability that the second child also received a ball?

Answer _____

(c) What is the probability that the first child was given a puzzle, the second a ball, and the third a puzzle?

Answer _____

3. Fifty men and 40 women are enrolled as graduate students in the Department of Psychology. Of the men, 25 are specializing in clinical, 15 in personality-social, and 10 in experimental psychology. Of the women, 25 are in clinical, 10 in personality-social, and 5 in experimental.

(a) Male experimental students make up what proportion of the total student body?

Answer _____

(b) Given a female student, what is the probability that she is in clinical?

Answer _____

(c) Given a personality-social student, what is the probability that the student is a man?

Answer _____

4. An experiment is to be conducted in which each subject's capacity to distinguish sounds is to be studied under three listening conditions. The order in which subjects experience the conditions is to vary. If every possible order were to be used with an equal number of subjects, what is the *minimum* number of subjects that would have to be tested?

Answer _____

5. A young business executive has 7 outfits she wears to work and does not want to wear the same outfit twice in one week. However, she often forgets what she wore when and decides to set up an order for what to wear during each 5-day workweek.

(a) Remembering her statistics class, she figures out how many permutations there would be. What is the number?

Answer _____

(b) How many combinations are there?

Answer _____

Section I

Problems for Chapter 7:
The Binomial and the Normal Distribution

I. TERMS AND SYMBOLS TO REVIEW

> Binomial probability distribution
> Binomial equation $[(p + q)^N]$
> Mean of binomial (μ_b)
> Standard deviation of binomial (σ_b)
> Normal probability distribution
> Inflection points

II. SHORT-ANSWER QUESTIONS

1. In the binomial situation, (a) _____ of _____ possible outcomes occurs on each of a number of (b) _____ occasions. The probability of the event designated as the favored event (or as a "hit") occurring on any occasion is symbolized as (c) _____. The probability of the nonfavored event (or "miss") is symbolized as (d) _____ and (e) _____ = 1.00.

2. By expanding the binomial equation (a) _____, it is possible to determine the probability of obtaining on N occasions the various numbers of hits from 0 to N. The list of probabilities is known as the (b) _____.

3. In the binomial expansion, the coefficient of each term corresponds to the

    (a) _____ of occurrence of the specified number of hits out of the total number of possible patterns of hits and misses on N occasions. Each term corresponds to the (b) _____ of occurrence.

4. The coefficient in each term in the binomial expansion can also be determined by finding the

    (a) _____ of (b) _____ things taken (c) _____ at a time, where (d) _____ is the number of hits.

5. The list of frequencies of the hits from 0 to N in a binomial probability distribution constitutes a frequency distribution whose mean and standard deviation can be determined in the usual way. The mean of the binomial distribution, which is symbolized as (a) _____, can also be determined by the formula (b) _____. The standard deviation, which is symbolized as (c) _____, can be determined by the formula (d) _____.

6. When $p = 1/2$, the shape of the binomial distribution is always (a) _____. As N increases, the shape of the binomial distribution increasingly resembles the shape of another theoretical distribution, (b) _____.

7. The binomial distribution is based on (a) _____ data and the normal probability distribution is based on (b) _____.

8. A card is to be selected at random from a bridge deck of 52 cards. If the favored event is a spade and the nonfavored event is any other suit, then p is equal to (a) _____ and q is equal to (b) _____.

9. The normal curve is one specific member of a family of symmetrical (a) _____ shaped curves. In a normal curve, the z scores of ± 1.00 fall at the (b) _____ points of the curve.

10. In every normal curve, the same proportion or percentage of the area under the curve lie between the (a) _____ and any given (b) _____. The percentage of the area between the mean and $z = +1.00$ is (c) _____. The percentage between $z \pm 1.00$ is therefore (d) _____.

11. The probability that an individual case drawn at random will fall between the mean and any given z score is the same as the proportion of _____ _____.

Answers

1. (a) one of two   (b) independent   (c) p (d) q (e) $p + q$ 2. (a) $(p + q)^N$ (b) binomial probability distribution   3. (a) frequency   (b) probability   4. (a) combination   (b) N (c) r (d) r 5. (a) μ_b (b) Np (c) σ_b (d) $\sqrt{Npq}$ 6. (a) symmetrical   (b) the normal probability distribution   7. (a) categorical (the favored event does or does not occur on each occasion)   (b) numerical   8. (a) 1/4   (b) 3/4   9. (a) bell   (b) inflection

10. (a) mean (μ)   (b) z score   (c) 34.13   (d) 68.26   11. the area under the curve between the
mean and the z score

III.   CALCULATIONAL PROBLEMS

1.   A coin is flipped 6 times.

   (a)   Using the multiplication rule, determine how many different
       patterns of heads (H) and tails (T) are possible and the
       probability of each.   _____

   (b)   How many patterns are there in which there are 4 H and 2 T?
       (Use Formula 7.2.)   _____

   (c)   What is the probability of obtaining 4 H and 2 T?   _____

   (d)   What is the mean of the distribution of frequencies?   _____

   (e)   What is the standard deviation of the distribution?   _____

2.   On each of 4 occasions, a card is selected from a deck of 52, its suit recorded, the card replaced
in the deck, and the deck reshuffled. A heart is called a hit and any other suit a miss.

   (a)   How many different patterns of hits and misses are there?
       (Use the multiplication rule.)   _____

   (b)   Are the probabilities of these patterns equal?   _____
   (c)   What is the probability of obtaining 2 hits and 2 misses, that is,
       2 hearts and 2 cards of two other suits? (Use Formula 7.2.)   _____

   (d)   What is the mean of the distribution?   _____

   (e)   What is the *variance* of the distribution?   _____

     The following problems require use of the normal curve table (Table B in the text). In finding
the answer, you may find it helpful first to draw a normal curve, add the information given, and
shade in the areas that the question concerns.

3.   What percentage of the area in a normal curve lies between the mean
    and z = –2.13?   _____
4.   What is the probability that a single case drawn at random from a
    normal distribution will lie between the μ and σ = –2.13?   _____
5.   What is the probability that an individual will score at or below
    z = –2.13?   _____
6.   What is the probability that an individual will score between
    z = ±.50?   _____

7.   The top 10% of the cases receive a z score of what or more?   _____

8.   In a normal distribution with μ = 140 and σ = 10:

   (a)   What is the percentile rank of X = 150?   _____

   (b)   What is the percentile rank of X = 135?   _____

   (c)   What is the probability that an individual scores 152 or *above*?   _____

   (d)   What is the probability that an individual scores at or between
       125 and 155?   _____

Answers

1. (a) In a set of 6 flips, there are $(2)^6 = 64$ possible patterns; with $p = 1/2$, each is equally probable: 1/64   (b) $C_4^6 = 6!/(4!)(6-4)! = 15$ (c) $15(1/2)^4(1/2)^2 = 15(1/16)(1/4) = 15/64 = .234$ (d) $6(1/2) = 3$ (e) $\sqrt{6(1/2)(1/2)} = 1.225$ 2. (a) with 2 possible outcomes, heart (H) and not a heart ($\bar{H}$); there are $2^4 = 16$ possible patterns   (b) no, since the probability of H and $\bar{H}$ are not equal   (c) C_2^4 $(1/4)^2(3/4)^2 = 6(1/16)(9/16) = 6(.0625)(.5625) = .2109$ (d) $4(1/4) = 1$ (e) $\sigma_b^2 = 4(1/4)(3/4) = .75$ 3. 48.34%   4. .4834   5. $.5000 - .4834 = .0166$ 6. $2(.1915) = .383$ 7. 40% of cases are between the mean and $z = 1.28$ and 10% beyond this z 8. (a) $z = (150-140)/10 = 1.00$; $50\% + 34.13\% = $ PR of 84.13   (b) $z = (135-140)/10 = -.50$; PR $= 50.00 - 19.15 = 30.85$ (c) $z = (152-140)/10 = 1.2$; $.5000 - .3849 = .1151$ (d) $z = (125-140)/10 = -1.5$ and $z = (155-140)/10 = +1.5$; $2(.4332) = .8664$

74

IV.   FURTHER EXERCISES

1. Six true-false questions appear on an examination that refer to material a student can't even recall reading. The student decides to answer each one by guessing. In answering the following questions, assume that the probability of the student's being correct on each item is .50.

   (a) Set up a theoretical frequency distribution of the number of correct guesses (from 0 to 6) that could be expected.

Correct	*Frequency*
6	_____
5	_____
4	_____
3	_____
2	_____
1	_____
0	$\Sigma f =$ _____

   (b) Graph the distribution of frequencies.

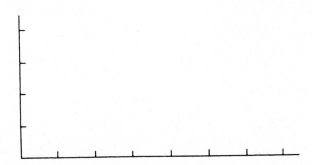

   (c) Using the data obtained in the table in (a), determine the probability that the student guessed correctly on 2 items.

                                        Answer _____

(d) Now obtain the frequency and probability of 2 correct guesses out of 6 by Formula 7.2. (Check to see that your answers correspond to what you found in (a) and (c) above.)

f _____

p _____

(e) Since the distribution of frequencies is symmetrical, it is easy to determine the mean of the distribution by inspection. Indicate the value of the mean by indicating its position on the baseline of the graph obtained in (b). Now calculate the mean by Formula 7.3. (Check to see if your two answers are the same.)

Answer _____

(f) Calculate the standard deviation of the distribution by Formula 7.5.

Answer _____

2. In a study of extrasensory perception, a signal was given to a subject to guess which of 4 cards, numbered 1–4, had just been pulled out at random in a room next door. This procedure was repeated 5 times.

The table below shows (in fractional form) some of the probabilities associated with various numbers of correct answers if the person had no ESP and was correct only by chance.

$p = .25$
$q = .75$
$N = 5$

Correct	p
5	1/1024
4	_____
3	90/1024
2	_____
1	405/1024
0	243/1024

(a)   Fill in the remaining probabilities.

(b)   What is the probability (in fractional form) that the person will guess correctly 3 *or more* times by chance alone?

Answer _____

(c)   What is the mean and standard deviation of the distribution?

μ_b _____

σ_b _____

(d)   After examining the table, state what happens to the shape of the probability distribution as p decreases from 1/2 toward 0 when N is small.

3.   The personnel department of a large manufacturing company has given a test of manual dexterity to a large number of applicants for positions in the assembly division. The results obtained from 500 men indicated that the frequency distribution of scores closely approximated the normal curve. The mean and standard deviation were as below:

Mean: 84
Standard deviation: 5
N = 500

(a)   Graph the results. Locate the mean and the points that are 1, 2, and 3 z score units above and below the mean. (Be sure to use the inflection points in locating $z = \pm1.00$.) Label the z score and the raw score values of each of these points. Consult the graph as you solve the remaining problems. (Draw your graph at the top of the next page.)

84

(b) What percentage of those tested scored 77 or *below*?

Answer _____

(c) How many of the 500 men scored 77 or below?

Answer _____

(d) How many scored between 79 and 89?

Answer _____

(e) What is the percentile rank of the score of 92?

Answer _____

(f) What is the raw score equivalent of the 30th percentile?

Answer _____

(g) The extreme 10% of the cases (5% at either end) had a raw score of what and below or a raw score of what and above?

Answer _____

(h) The middle 80% of the cases had raw scores between what values?

Answer _____

(i) What is the probability that a score drawn at random falls between 82 and 86?

Answer _____

4. The company (in problem 3) has also tested 400 women on the same test of manual dexterity. Their data are given below. The men's data (from problem 3) are also given.

	Women	Men
Mean:	86	84
Standard deviation:	4	5
N:	400	500

(a) What is the probability that a woman scored at or above the mean of the men?

Answer _____

(b) A man earned a score of 89. To have the same percentile rank in the distribution of women's scores, a woman would have to score what?

Answer _____

(c) What proportion of the women scored at or *below* the mean of the women but at or *above* the mean of the men?

Answer _____

Section J

Problems for Chapter 8:
Sampling Distributions: Single Samples

I.   TERMS AND SYMBOLS TO REVIEW

Sampling distribution	Two-tailed test
Standard error of $\bar{X}$ ($\sigma_{\bar{X}}$)	One-tailed test
Estimated standard error of $\bar{X}$ ($s_{\bar{X}}$)	Type I (α) error
Central limit theorem	Type II (β) error
Null hypothesis (H_0)	Confidence interval for μ
Alternative hypothesis (H_1)	Standard error of proportion (σ_{prop})

II.   SHORT-ANSWER QUESTIONS

1.   A sampling distribution is a mathematical model that represents the distribution of

(a) _____

_____.

The sampling distribution of $\bar{X}$ represents the distribution of (b) _____

_____

_____.

2. When the size of each sample is large, the shape of the sampling distribution of $\bar{X}$'s approximates the (a) _____. When the mean of the distribution of $\bar{X}$'s is found, its value is equal to the value of the (b) _____.

3. The standard deviation of the theoretical sampling distribution of $\bar{X}$'s is called the
    (a) _____ of the mean and is symbolized as
    (b) _____. The value of this standard deviation has been shown to be equal to the quantity (c) _____.

4. As sample size grows larger, the size of the standard error of the mean grows
    (a) _____ and the shape of the distribution of $\bar{X}$'s increasingly resembles the (b) _____. These relationships make up the
    (c) _____ theorem.

5. The standard error of the mean when estimated from the data of a sample is symbolized as
    (a) _____ and is obtained by substituting (b) _____ for (c) _____
    in the standard error formula. This procedure of estimating an exact value for a population parameter is known as (d) _____.

6. In testing a hypothesis about μ, one first sets up a (a) _____ hypothesis, symbolized as (b) _____, which specifies an exact value for μ. Then one sets up an
    (c) _____ hypothesis, symbolized as (d) _____, which specifies that (e) _____.

7. A bidirectional H_1 specifies that μ is (a) _____
    _____ and a unidirectional H_1 specifies that (b) _____
    _____.

8. In testing a null hypothesis (H_0) about μ, the sample $\bar{X}$ is converted into an estimated z score, identified as _____.

9. If H_1 is bidirectional, a (a) _____ tailed test is performed in which the probability is determined of obtaining (b) _____
    _____.

10. When samples are large, the shape of the t distribution may be assumed to be
    (a) _____. When samples are small and the population is normal, the t
    distribution is (b) _____ in shape but (c) _____ than the
    normal curve. Its exact shape is related to the number of (d) _____
    associated with the sample.

11. The probability levels used to evaluate H_0 are known as (a) _____ or
    (b) _____ levels. The specific levels typically used in scientific research are
    (c) _____ and (d) _____.

12. If the calculated value of t equals or exceeds the value of t associated with a specified α level, the null hypothesis is (a) _____ and the alternative hypothesis is (b) _____.

13. When H_0 is rejected at a given alpha level and it is in fact true, a Type (a) _____ or (b) _____ error has occurred. The probability of this type of error occurring is equal to (c) _____.

14. When H_0 is not rejected at a given α level and it is in fact false, a Type (a) _____ or (b) _____ error has occurred. The probability of this type of error is (c) _____, its value typically being (d) _____ than α.

15. When the sample N is large, the value of t associated with the specified alpha level can be found in the (a) _____ table. When the sample N is small, the critical value of t for the specified alpha level is found in the (b) _____, and is associated with the number of (c) _____ in the sample.

16. The ability of a statistical test to detect a false H_0 and reduce the incidence of Type II errors is known as the (a) _____ of the test. As sample N increases, power (b) _____.

17. When investigators have no specific hypothesis about the value of μ, they may choose to set up a (a) _____ for μ. This involves setting up a (b) _____ within which it is asserted at a certain probability level that μ falls. Two probability levels are commonly used, resulting in the (c) _____ and _____ CI's.

18. In a binomial situation, the proportion of individuals in a population who fall into one category is identified as p and the proportion who fall into the second category is identified as q. Assuming a sufficiently large sample size, the binomial distribution of p values obtained from an infinite number of random samples approximates the shape of the (a) _____ based on (b) _____ measures. The mean of the sampling distribution of p's takes the same value as the population (c) _____. The standard deviation of the sampling distribution of p is called the (d) _____ of the (e) _____, symbolized as (f) _____.

19. A null hypothesis about a population proportion (p) may be tested by converting an obtained sample p into a (a) _____ in the theoretical normal distribution to be expected if H_0 is true. If its value equals or exceeds the value associated with the specified alpha level, H_0 is (b) _____.

Answers

1. (a) the values of a sample statistic that would be obtained from an infinite number of random samples of a given size   (b) the values of $\overline{X}$ obtained from an infinite number of random samples   2. (a) normal probability distribution   (b) population mean or μ 3. (a) standard error   (b) $\sigma_{\overline{X}}$ (c) $\sigma/\sqrt{N}$ 4. (a) smaller   (b) normal curve   (c) central limit   5. (a) $s_{\overline{X}}$ (b) s (c) σ (d) point estimation   6. (a) null   (b) H_0 (c) alternative   (d) H_1 (e) μ is some value other than the value specified in H_0 7. (a) unequal to the value in H_0 (b) either that μ is greater than specified in H_0 or that it is less than that value   8. t 9. (a) two   (b) $\overline{X}$ that deviates as much or more in either direction from the μ specified in H_0 (c) $\overline{X}$ that deviates as much or more from the μ in H_0 in the direction specified in H_1 10. (a) normal   (b) symmetrical   (c) flatter   (d) degrees of freedom (df)   11. (a) significance   (b) alpha (α)   (c) .05 (or 5%)   (d) .01 (or 1%)   12. (a) rejected   (b) accepted   13. (a) I   (b) α (c) α 14. (a) II   (b) beta (β)   (c) β (d) greater than α 15. (a) normal curve   (b) t table   (c) degrees of freedom (df)   16. (a) power   (b) increases   17. (a) confidence interval   (b) range of values   (c) 95% and 99%   18. (a) normal distribution   (b) continuous   (c) p or proportion   (d) standard error   (e) proportion   (f) σ_{prop} 19. (a) z score   (b) rejected

III. MULTIPLE-CHOICE QUESTIONS

_____ 1. The mean and standard deviation of a population are known to be 69 and 10, respectively. If an infinite number of random samples of 25 cases each were drawn from the population and the $\overline{X}$'s obtained: (a) in theory, the mean of the sampling distribution of $\overline{X}$'s could be found by summing the $\overline{X}$'s and dividing by the number of samples   (b) the mean of the sampling distribution would be equal to 69   (c) the standard error would be equal to 2   (d) all the above are correct   (e) none of the above is correct.

_____ 2. In a sampling distribution of $\overline{X}$'s based on samples of 200 cases each, the standard error is 1. The μ of the population is 40. The probability that a sample $\overline{X}$ takes a value between 39 and 41 is approximately: (a) .34   (b) .68   (c) .98   (d) can't tell without additional information.

_____ 3. Two random samples, one of 20 cases and one of 100 cases, have been drawn from the same population and happen to have the same $\overline{X}$ and s.   (a) the mean of the two theoretical sampling distributions of $\overline{X}$'s associated with the two samples is larger for the larger sample   (b) the mean of the two theoretical sampling distributions of $\overline{X}$'s is smaller for the distribution associated with the larger sample   (c) the standard error of $\overline{X}$ is the same for both sampling distributions   (d) the standard error is larger for the sampling distribution associated with the larger sample   (e) the means of the two sampling distributions are the same but the standard error is smaller for the sampling distribution associated with the larger sample.

_____ 4. When the population is normal, the shape of the t distribution: (a) is symmetrical   (b) is flatter than the normal distribution   (c) varies with df (d) all the above are correct.

_____ 5. A hypothesis is tested about μ with a bidirectional H_1. The critical value of t is 2.03 and the computed t is 2.10.   (a) H_0 should not be rejected   (b) H_0 should be rejected   (c) H_1 should be rejected   (d) none of the above.

_____ 6. Using $\alpha = .01$, an investigator tests H_0: $\mu = 40$ and H_1: $\mu < 40$. His sample $\overline{X}$ turns out to be 43.   (a) H_0 should immediately be accepted   (b) H_0 should immediately be rejected   (c) H_1 should be changed to a bidirectional hypothesis and t computed   (d) no conclusions are possible without computing t.

_____ 7. The null hypothesis that investigators test: (a) sometimes coincides with their actual research hypothesis   (b) always coincides with their research hypothesis   (c) never coincides with their research hypothesis.

8. The 99% CI for μ, in contrast to the 95% CI: (a) specifies a smaller range of values for μ (b) has a greater probability of including the value of μ (c) is uninfluenced by sample size   (d) has a smaller probability of including the value of μ (e) none of the above is correct.

9. H_0 is rejected at the .05 significance level. The probability that an erroneous conclusion has been reached is: (a) greater than .05   (b) equal to β (c) equal to .05   (d) less than .05   (e) both (a) and (b) are correct.

10. H_0 is accepted at the .01 significance level. The probability that an erroneous conclusion has been reached is: (a) greater than .01   (b) equal to β (c) equal to .01   (d) less than .01   (e) both (a) and (b) are correct.

11. In the binomial situation, the mean of the sampling distribution of sample proportions is equal to: (a) the mean of the population   (b) the population proportion   (c) Np where N is equal to sample size   (d) all the above are correct.

12. In testing a hypothesis about a population proportion, z is computed rather than t because: (a) the shape of the theoretical sampling distribution of sample proportions approximates the normal curve   (b) the value of the standard error of proportion for the sampling distribution expected under H_0 does not have to be estimated   (c) large samples are used   (d) t is used only to test a hypothesis about μ.

Answers

1. (d)   2. (b)   3. (e)   4. (d)   5. (b)   6. (a)   7. (a)   8. (b)   9. (c)
10. (e)   11. (b)   12. (b)

IV. CALCULATIONAL PROBLEMS

1. In a sample of 256 cases, $\overline{X}$ is 62 and s is 8. The hypotheses to be tested are: $H_0: \mu = 63$ and $H_1: \mu \neq 63$. Alpha is set at .05.

    (a)   Determine $s_{\overline{X}}$.   _____

    (b)   Determine t.   _____

    (c)   Determine df.   _____

    (d)   What is the critical value of t for the specified μ and H_1?   _____

    (e)   Should you reject or not reject H_0?   _____

2. In a sample of 25 cases, $\overline{X} = 74$ and s = 10. $H_0: \mu = 76$ and $H_1: \mu < 76$, $\alpha = .01$.

    (a)   Determine $s_{\overline{X}}$.   _____

    (b)   Determine t.   _____

    (c)   Determine df.   _____

    (d)   What is the critical value of t for the specified μ and H_1?   _____

    (e)   Should you reject or not reject H_0?   _____

3. In a sample of 196 cases, $\bar{X} = 150$ and $s = 21$. The 95% confidence interval (CI) for μ is to be established.

   (a) Determine $s_{\bar{X}}$. _____

   (b) What is the value of t to be used in the equation for the 95% CI? _____

   (c) What is the range of values for the CI? _____

4. In a sample of 36 cases, $\bar{X} = 49$ and $s = 9$. The 99% CI is to be established.

   (a) Determine $s_{\bar{X}}$. _____

   (b) Determine df. _____

   (c) What is the value of t? _____

   (d) What is the range of values for this CI? _____

5. In a sample of 20 individuals, 12 fell into one category ($p_s = .60$) and 8 fell into a second category ($q_s = .40$). H_0 is that the population p is .50 and H_1 is bidirectional. Use $\alpha = .05$ to evaluate H_0.

   (a) Determine σ_{prop}. _____

   (b) Determine z. _____

   (c) What is the value of z in testing H_0? _____

   (d) Should you reject or not reject H_0? _____

Answers

1. (a) $8/\sqrt{256} = .5$ (b) $t = (62 - 63)/.5 = -2.00$ (c) $df = 256 - 1 = 255$ (d) with a sample this large, use normal curve value: $t_{.05} = 1.96$ (e) since the absolute value of the computed t exceeds the critical value, reject H_0 at $\alpha = .05$

2. (a) $10/\sqrt{25} = 2$ (b) $t = (74 - 76)/2 = -1.00$ (c) $df = 24$ (d) With a unidirectional H_1, a one-tailed test may be used; $t_{.01}$ (one-tailed) $= 2.49$.   (e) cannot reject

3. (a) $21/\sqrt{196} = 1.5$ (b) for a large sample, $t_{.05} = 1.96$ (c) 95% CI $= 150 \pm 1.96 \, (1.5) = 147.06$ to 152.94

4. (a) $9/\sqrt{36} = 1.5$ (b) $df = 35$ (c) $t_{.01} = 2.72$ (d) 99% CI: $49 \pm 2.72 \, (1.5) = 44.92$ to 53.08

5. (a) $\sigma_{prop} = \sqrt{(.5)\,(.5)/20} = .112$ (Note that p and q are the hypothesized population values.)
(b) $z = (.60 - .50)/.112 = .893$ (c) $z_{.05} = 1.96$ (d) cannot reject

V.   FURTHER EXERCISES

1.   An entire population of individuals was measured and the distribution of scores was found to be normal. The mean and standard deviation were calculated to be

$$\mu = 84$$
$$\sigma = 10$$

(a)   Random samples of 4 cases each are drawn from the population. Find the standard error of the mean ($\sigma_{\bar{X}}$) for the sampling distribution of $\bar{X}$'s when the sample N's are 4.

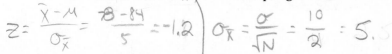

$Z = \dfrac{\bar{X} - M}{\sigma_{\bar{X}}} = \dfrac{78 - 84}{5} = -1.2$ $\sigma_{\bar{X}} = \dfrac{\sigma}{\sqrt{N}} = \dfrac{10}{2} = 5.5$

Answer _____

38.49
+50.00
_____
88.49

(b)   Find $\sigma_{\bar{X}}$ for the sampling distribution in which the samples each consist of 64 cases.

$$\sigma_{\bar{X}} = \dfrac{10}{8} = 1.25$$

Answer _____

(c)   Find $\sigma_{\bar{X}}$ for the sampling distribution in which the samples each consist of 400 cases.

$$\sigma_{\bar{X}} = \dfrac{10}{20} = .50$$

Answer _____

(d)   sketch the
Shown below is a frequency polygon representing the distribution of scores in the population. On the same graph, sketch the frequency polygons for the sampling distribution of $\bar{X}$'s in which sample N's are 4 and 400. (Use the graph in considering your answer to the next question.

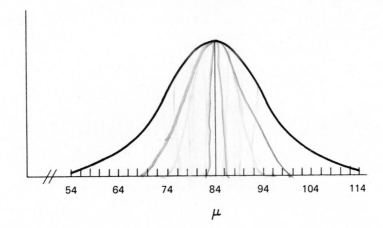

(e) As sample sizes grow larger and larger, approaching the population N, the $\sigma_{\bar{X}}$ of the sampling distribution of $\bar{X}$'s approaches what value? As sample size decreases, approaching N = 1, $\sigma_{\bar{X}}$ approaches what value?

Answer _____

2. Scores on an aptitude test are available for all applicants for Civil Service positions and constitute a population of scores. The scores are normally distributed and have a mean of 134 and a standard deviation of 24.

(a) Graph the sampling distribution of $\bar{X}$'s that would be expected if an infinite number of random samples of 36 cases each were drawn from the population. Indicate the mean and standard error on the graph.

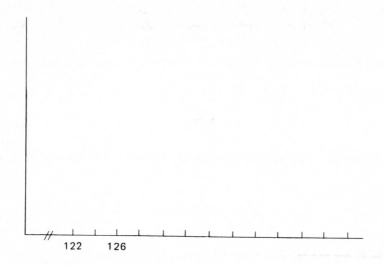

(b) What is the probability of drawing a single sample whose $\bar{X}$ is 137 or greater? Show your solution graphically in the polygon you drew in (a) above.

Answer _____

(c)   What is the probability of drawing a sample of 36 cases whose $\bar{X}$ differs from μ by 5 or more score units *in either direction*? (Picturing the problem in the polygon in (a) may help you in finding the answer.)

Answer _____

3.   An investigation is performed in which subjects are required to adjust the brightness of a lighted panel until it appears to them to match a standard comparison panel whose brightness is fixed. The investigator arranges the viewing conditions in such a way that he suspects a perceptual illusion will occur, such that subjects will tend to adjust the variable panel so that it is *brighter* than the standard panel. However, he has no idea about how large the perceptual illusion is, if it exists. The brightness of the standard is 60 units. The mean of the subjects' setting of the variable stimulus and other sample statistics are shown below.

$$H_0 : M = 60$$
$$H_1 : M > 60$$

t-test $\bar{X} = 61.9$

$s = 5.5$

$N = 25$

(a)   What null hypothesis about μ should the investigator test?

+alternative

Answer _____

(b)   What is $s_{\bar{X}}$ for the sampling distribution of $\bar{X}$'s?

Answer _____

(c)   Test H_0, using $\alpha = .05$ and a bidirectional H_1. After stating whether or not you reject H_0, come to a concrete conclusion about what was demonstrated in *this particular experiment*.

$$H_1 : M \neq 60$$

89

(d) Your conclusion in (c) could be in error. Identify which type (I or II) this error would be and state the approximate probability of its occurrence.

Answer _____

(e) If you wanted to minimize the probability of this type of error, would you raise α to .01 or lower it to .10?

Answer _____

(f) Suppose that the investigator had decided to test H_0 and a unidirectional H_1. In light of his experimental hypothesis, what would this H_1 be?

$H_1: M > 60$

Answer _____

(g) With the H_1 specified in (f) and $\alpha = .05$, what would he conclude about H_0?

Answer _____

(h) His conclusion could be in error. What type of error would it be?

Answer _____

4. A health organization has obtained a number of measures of physical fitness from a random sample of 64 men in this country who are 50–54 years of age. On a measure of lung capacity, the following data are obtained:

$$\Sigma X = 960 \qquad \Sigma X^2 = 15{,}408 \qquad N = 64$$

(a) What are the two scores that define the limits of the 95% confidence interval for μ of the population from which the sample was drawn?

Answer _____

90

(b) What are the score limits of the 99% confidence interval?

Answer _____

5. A much-debated amendment to the city code is to be voted upon at a special election and requires a two-thirds majority to pass. The day before the election, a newspaper reporter selects 100 persons at random from the list of registered voters and asks them how they plan to vote. Of the 100, 65 say that they will vote "yes" and 35 say they will vote "no." Assuming that people do not change their opinions, should the reporter predict that the amendment will fail or that it may well pass? Answer the question after performing the appropriate statistical test.

Section K

Special Review:

Hypothesis Testing

Test yourself with the following questions about sampling distributions without looking up the answers in the text. Assuming that the sample N's are large and samples have been randomly selected:

1. The shape of the sampling distribution of $\overline{X}$'s approximates what theoretical distribution? The mean of the sampling distribution of $\overline{X}$'s is equal to the value of what population parameter?
2. In the binomial situation, the shape of the sampling distribution of sample proportions (p) approximates what theoretical distribution? The mean of the sampling distribution of p's is equal to the value of what population parameter?
3. The shape of the sampling distribution of sample s^2's approximates what theoretical distribution? The mean of the sampling distribution is equal to the value of what population parameter?

These questions have a repetitive quality to them and most students have no difficulty in correctly saying that all three of the theoretical sampling distributions approximate the normal distribution when samples are sufficiently large. Most students also readily state that the mean of the sampling distribution of sample means ($\overline{X}$'s) takes the same value as the mean of the population, μ.

Many students answer that in the binomial situation, the mean of the sampling distribution of sample proportions (p's) is also equal to μ (and then, if they answer at all, go on to give the same answer about the mean of the sampling distribution of s^2's). However, the correct answer in the second problem is the population proportion and in the third problem it is the population σ^2. Failure to answer these questions correctly reflects a confusion that seriously interferes with understanding the basic logic of hypothesis testing that applies not only to tests of hypotheses about the population parameters discussed in Chapter 8 of the text, but also to tests of hypotheses about additional population parameters, some of which are discussed in later chapters. In this special review, an attempt will be made to clear up the confusion and get everyone back on track.

Where Students Go Wrong and How to Avoid It

The statistical tests that are considered in the text are applied to three major types of data. One of these involves a set of two or more mutually exclusive categories in which each individual in a group is assigned to a category and the *proportion* of the individuals that fall into each category is determined. In the binomial situation, individuals are classified into one of two categories, the proportion in one being identified as p and the proportion in the other being identified as q.

Numerical data, on the other hand, involve assigning to each individual in a group a number that indicates how much of some property the individual exhibits. A variety of statistics have been devised to describe the distribution of a group of measures—the mean, standard deviation, and so forth. And finally there are rank order data in which individuals are ordered according to the amount of some property they exhibit.

These distinctions should be quite obvious but in practice, students often forget them or ignore them, with unfortunate results. In trying to understand the logic of a particular statistical test or in deciding what kind of hypothesis to test with a specific set of data:

Rule 1. Identify the type of data and the particular statistic in question.

The second point to remember may seem too obvious to mention but it turns out that it is not. If one has a series of N quantities, one can add them up and divide by N to obtain their mean. It is important to remember what these quantities, and thus their mean, represent. For example, if you measured individuals' height in inches and determined the mean, it is perfectly apparent to you that the mean represents *height in inches* of the average individual in the group, not pounds, IQ score, or proportion of redheads. But when the quantities whose mean is being obtained are more abstract than in this example, students often lose sight of what the mean represents. For example, one could find the proportion of women (p) and men (q) in each of a large number of samples. The basic data, then, are *categorical*. Since a p value has been found for each sample, a series of quantities has been generated whose mean can be determined by adding up the sample p's and dividing the sum by the number of p values. The result is the mean *proportion* (p), the average *proportion* of women in the collection of samples. In like manner, one could measure individuals' height in each of a number of samples, and then compute the $\bar{X}$ of each sample. The mean of this collection of $\bar{X}$'s represents the average $\bar{X}$. Or one could obtain s^2 for each sample and then determine the mean s^2, and so forth.

Rule 2. When the mean of a series of quantities has been obtained, always identify what the quantities are and thus what the mean of these quantities represents.

We're now ready to tackle directly the question of the means of sampling distributions and what population parameter they equal. Starting with an example, suppose that we are concerned with a binomial situation and have a population in which $p = .50$. If we draw an infinite number of random samples of, let us say, 100 cases each, we anticipate that in some of the samples, p would be less than .50 and in others it would be greater than .50. Statistical theory tells us that these overestimates and underestimates of the population p cancel each other out, so that the average of the sample p values would be .50. In other words, the mean of the sampling distribution of sample *proportions* would be equal to the population *proportion*, which in this example is .50. (You now see why the mean of the sample p's couldn't be equal to the population μ, as many students are prone to say. The population doesn't even have a mean since the basic data are categorical.)

Or suppose that we have measured individuals in each of a large number of random samples and have obtained s^2 for each sample, that is, an unbiased estimate of the population variance or σ^2. Some of the sample s^2's would be smaller than σ^2 and others would be larger than σ^2. Their mean—that is, the mean of the sampling distribution of s^2's—would be equal to the population σ^2.

What about the sampling distribution of $\bar{X}$'s? Some sample $\bar{X}$'s are larger than the population μ and some are smaller. The mean of the sampling distribution of $\bar{X}$'s would be equal to the parallel population parameter, μ.

These are only three examples of sampling distributions of particular statistics. In later chapters in the text, other sampling distributions will be discussed, for example, the sampling distribution of Pearson's r's. What statistical theory tells us is that (providing certain assumptions are met[1]) the mean of the distribution of any given sample statistic takes the same value as the *equivalent population parameter*. If the sample statistic is a *proportion*, then the mean of the sample proportions takes the value of the population *proportion*; if the sample statistic is a *mean* ($\bar{X}$), then the mean of the sample $\bar{X}$'s is equal to the population parameter that is parallel to $\bar{X}$, that is, the *mean* of the population or μ, and so forth. To express this relationship briefly:

Rule 3. The mean of the sampling distribution of some statistic takes the same value as the population parameter that is the equivalent of that statistic.

General Logic of Sampling Distributions

Once you understand the relationship between the mean of the sampling distribution of some statistic and the parallel population parameter, you should be able to understand the general logic behind most of the statistical tests presented in the text. Assuming that certain assumptions are met, statistical theory allows us:

1. To specify the shape of the theoretical sampling distribution of the given statistic, that is, the shape of the distribution of values that would be obtained if we found the value of the statistic for each of an infinite number of random samples drawn from the specified population. In many instances, this distribution approximates the normal distribution but not always. The essential point, however, is that the form and hence the mathematical properties of the distribution are known.
2. To state that the mean of the theoretical sampling distribution of a statistic has the same value as the population parameter that is parallel to that statistic.
3. To determine the standard error (i.e., the standard deviation) of the sampling distribution, given certain information about the population and sample N's.

With knowledge of the shape of a sampling distribution and the value of its mean and standard error, it is possible to make probability statements about the likelihood of obtaining samples whose values deviate as much or more from the value of the population parameter by any special amount or more. For example, in a binomial situation, we can determine the probability of obtaining a p of .55 or greater or of .45 or less in a sample of a given size when the population p is .50.

---

[1]The particular assumptions underlying each type of statistical test are outlined in the text. One of them is that the statistic obtained from a sample is an unbiased or nearly unbiased estimate of the population parameter.

General Logic of Statistical Tests

We seldom have data from entire populations and would have no need of obtaining samples if we did. However, it is possible to use our theoretical knowledge about sampling distributions to set up and test a hypothesis (null hypothesis or H_0) about an unknown population parameter, based on the data from a single sample. The reasoning we use is as follows:

1. The approximate shape of the sampling distribution is known.
2. If the hypothesis (H_0) about the population parameter we are testing is true, the mean of the hypothetical sampling distribution is known (i.e., it is equal to the value of the population parameter specified in H_0).
3. The standard error of the hypothetical sampling distribution either can be determined or can be estimated from the sample data by use of the appropriate formula.
4. With knowledge of the mean, standard error, and shape of the hypothetical sampling distribution, statements can be made about the probability of obtaining a sample that deviated as much or more from H_0 as the obtained sample, if H_0 were true.
5. On the basis of this probability, a decision can be made about whether to reject H_0 as being unreasonable and to accept instead an alternative hypothesis about the population parameter, or to retain H_0 as being reasonable.

These statements about hypothesis testing constitute only the "bare bones" and are by no means complete. Understanding them, however, should allow you to assimilate the details of testing a hypothesis about a particular population parameter without losing sight of the basic statistical logic.

A Look Ahead

You should now be ready to move on to reading and solving problems for Chapter 9 of the text, which discusses, first, another type of sampling distribution, the difference between pairs of sample $\bar{X}$'s, the members of each pair being drawn from a different population; and second, a test of a null hypothesis about the difference between the equivalent population parameters—the difference between the μ's of the two populations ($\mu_1 - \mu_2$).

But first test yourself on this question (without consulting Chapter 9). The means ($\bar{X}$'s) of pairs of random samples (one from Population 1 and one from Population 2) are obtained, and then the difference is found between each pair of sample $\bar{X}$'s ($\bar{X}_1 - \bar{X}_2$). The mean of the sampling distribution of differences between pairs of $\bar{X}$'s is equal to what population value? If you answered, "the difference between the population μ's ($\mu_1 - \mu_2$)," give yourself a pat on the back and go ahead with Chapter 9. If you couldn't come up with the right answer, read over the material in this Special Review again and try to figure out why the current answer is $\mu_1 - \mu_2$.

● **Section L**

Problems for Chapter 9:

Sampling Distributions: Independent Samples from Two Populations

● **I.   TERMS AND SYMBOLS TO REVIEW**

Independent variable	Estimated standard error of the
Dependent variable	difference $(s_{\bar{x}_1 - \bar{x}_2})$
Experimental and control groups	H_0 about difference between μ's
Sampling distribution of	t ratio
differences between $\bar{X}$'s	t table
Standard error of the difference	Type I (α) and Type II (β) errors
between $\bar{X}$'s $(\sigma_{\bar{x}_1 - \bar{x}_2})$	Power of a test $(1 - \beta)$

II.   SHORT-ANSWER QUESTIONS

1. The subjects in an experiment are shown either a 5-minute film on a neutral topic or a humorous film of the same length. Next all subjects are asked to study a list of affectively pleasant words and then to recall them. Number of words recalled is determined for each subject. In this experiment, subjects shown the neutral film constitute the

   (a) _____ group and subjects shown the comedy constitute the

   (b) _____ group. Type of film is the

(c) _____ variable and number of words recalled is the

(d) _____ variable.

2. When experimental conditions have no differential effects, the μ's of the hypothetical populations of individuals observed under the several conditions take the

(a) _____ value. When the conditions do have differential effects, the values of the μ's are (b) _____.

3. When sample N's are large, the shape of the sampling distribution of the difference between pairs of sample means $(\bar{X}_1 - \bar{X}_2)$ approximates (a) _____.

When N's are small, its shape varies according to (b) _____.

4. The mean of the sampling distribution of the differences between $\bar{X}$'s takes the same value as (a) _____. The standard deviation of the distribution is called the

(b) _____ and is symbolized as (c) _____. An estimate of this standard deviation, based on the data from a single pair of samples, is symbolized as

(d) _____.

5. The null hypothesis (H_0) that is conventionally tested about the difference between μ's is that _____.

6. When t is calculated for the data from a pair of samples and is found to exceed the critical value of t at the specified α level, H_0 is (a) _____ at that level and it is concluded that (b) _____. If the calculated value of t is less than the critical value, H_0 is (c) _____.

7. In a two-group experiment, degrees of freedom (df) equals _____.

8. When N's are equal in a pair of samples, the standard errors of the mean that enter into the formula for $s_{\bar{X}_1 - \bar{X}_2}$ have (a) _____ weights. When sample N's are small and unequal, the formula for $s_{\bar{X}_1 - \bar{X}_2}$ must be modified in order to (b) _____

_____.

9. The use of a t test to test a hypothesis about the difference between μ's is based on two assumptions about the populations from which the samples were drawn. These are that

(a) _____ and that (b) _____

_____.

10. In a two-group experiment, the variability among the total groups of scores comes from two sources: (a) systematic differences between (a) _____ and (b) _____

_____. The first (systematic) source is reflected by (c) _____ in the

(d) _____ of the t ratio and the second source is reflected by

(e) _____ in the (f) _____ of the t ratio.

11. The power of a statistical test is defined as (a) _____

_____ and its value is determined by the formula (b) _____

_____. With a given H_1 and α level, the two major factors that influence the power of a test are (c) _____ and (d) _____. The latter, in turn, has two components, size of sample (e) _____ and (f) _____.

12. When H_1 is unidirectional, the power of a statistical test is _____ than when it is bidirectional.

13. The statistic $\hat{\omega}^2$ is an estimate of (a) _____ and is expressed in terms of an estimate of the proportion (b) _____

_____.

Answers

1. (a) control   (b) experimental   (c) independent   (d) dependent   2. (a) same
(b) different   3. (a) the normal curve   (b) df 4. (a) $\mu_1 - \mu_2$ (b) standard error of the
difference between means   (c) $\sigma_{\bar{X}_1 - \bar{X}_2}$ (d) $s_{\bar{X}_1 - \bar{X}_2}$ 5. $\mu_1 - \mu_2 = 0$ 6. (a) rejected
(b) the μ's are not the same   (c) not rejected   7. $(N_1 - 1) + (N_2 - 1)$ or $N_1 + N_2 - 2$
8. (a) equal   (b) to give greater weight to the larger sample   9. (a) the characteristic in
question is normally distributed in each of the populations   (b) the population σ's are equal
10. (a) means   (b) error   (c) $\bar{X}_1 - \bar{X}_2$ (d) numerator   (e) $s_{\bar{X}_1 - \bar{X}_2}$ (f) denominator
11. (a) the probability of detecting a false H_0 (b) $1 - p$ (Type II error) $= 1 - \beta$ (c) size of
difference between μ's   (d) size of $\sigma_{\bar{X}_1 - \bar{X}_2}$ (e) N's   (f) size of population σ's   12. greater
13. (a) effect size   (b) of the variability in scores that can be accounted for by the independent
(experimental) variable.

III.   MULTIPLE-CHOICE QUESTIONS

_____ 1. The t used to test the null hypothesis that population means are equal: (a) is a ratio between the difference between $\bar{X}$'s and the estimated standard error of the difference between means   (b) is an estimated z score   (c) must be evaluated by comparing it with a critical value of t at the specified α level   (d) permits rejection of H_0 when its value is greater than the critical value   (e) all of the above.

_____ 2. In an experiment in which there are two groups of 10 cases each, the df used to find the critical value of t is: (a) 9   (b) 10   (c) 15   (d) 18   (e) 20.

_____ 3. An experimenter tests H_0: $\mu_1 - \mu_2 = 0$ and the unidirectional H_1 that $\mu_1 > \mu_2$. After performing the experiment, he finds that $\bar{X}_1$ is 45.6 and $\bar{X}_2$ is 49.3.   (a) he retains H_0 and rejects H_1 (b) he rejects H_0 (c) he computes t before making a decision about H_0 (d) he must use a different df for evaluating t than if H_1 were bidirectional   (e) his use of a unidirectional H_1 decreased the power of the test. (Hint: Note what H_1 states about the difference.)

_____ 4. It is preferable to state that H_0 cannot be rejected rather than that H_0 is accepted because: (a) one can prove that H_0 is wrong but not that it is right   (b) one is less certain that one is correct when it is decided to retain H_0 than when it is decided to reject it   (c) the language is more symmetrical   (d) all of the above   (e) none of the above.

_____ 5. The power of a statistical test: (a) refers to the probability of making a Type I error   (b) increases with increases in sample variability   (c) increases with

increases in sample N   (d) is the same for bidirectional and unidirectional H_1's
(e) all of the above.

Answers

1. (e)   2. (d)   3. (a)   4. (b)   5. (c)

IV.   CALCULATIONAL PROBLEMS

1. An investigator has developed two parallel forms of a test that he intends to be equally difficult. He gives one form to one group and the second to another group and plans to compare the $\bar{X}$'s by a t test. The results are as follows:

$$\bar{X}_1 = 64 \qquad\qquad \bar{X}_2 = 62$$
$$s_{\bar{X}_1} = 3 \qquad\qquad s_{\bar{X}_2} = 4$$
$$N_1 = 16 \qquad\qquad N_2 = 16$$

(a) Set up H_0 and H_1.

H_0 _____

H_1 _____

(b) Find $s_{\bar{X}_1 - \bar{X}_2}$.

Answer _____

(c) Find t.

Answer _____

(d) Find df.

Answer _____

100

(e) Using $\alpha = .05$, what do you conclude about H_0?

Answer _____

(f) Restate your conclusion in terms of the specific question the investigator had in conducting the study.

2. A psychologist speculates that people who are proficient in learning foreign languages are able to distinguish sounds better than less proficient individuals. She selects individuals from an advanced course in conversational French, dividing them into two groups (High, Low) on the basis of teacher ratings of their fluency. Subjects are given a dichotic listening task consisting of a series of word pairs in which one word is heard over an earphone in one ear and another word is simultaneously heard in the other ear (e.g., shin, heat). The number of pairs in which both words are correctly reported is determined for each subject. The group results are as follows:

Group I (High)	Group 2 (Low)
$\bar{X}_H = 25.6$	$\bar{X}_L = 20.2$
$s_H = 4$	$s_L = 5$
$N_H = 10$	$N_L = 10$

(a) Set up H_0 and H_1.

H_0 _____

H_1 _____

(b) Compute $s_{\bar{X}_1 - \bar{X}_2}$.

Answer _____

(c) Compute t.

Answer _____

101

(d)   What do you conclude about the experimenter's hypothesis?

Answer _____

(e)   Estimate effect size.

Answer _____

Answers

1. (a) $H_0: \mu_1 - \mu_2 = 0$; $H_1: \mu_1 - \mu_2 \neq 0$ (b) $s\,\bar{x}_1 - \bar{x}_2 = \sqrt{3^2 + 4^2} = 5$ (c) $t = (64 - 62)/5 = .40$ (d) $df = 16 + 16 - 2 = 30$ (e) for $df = 30$, $t_{.05} = 2.04$; computed t is less than this value, so H_0 cannot be rejected   (f) the two test forms are equally difficult

2. (a) $H_0: \mu_H - \mu_L = 0$; H_1 could either be $\mu_H - \mu_L \neq 0$ (bidirectional) or the unidirectional hypothesis that $\mu_H > \mu_L$ (b) $(s\bar{x}_H)^2 = 16/10 = 1.6$; $(s\bar{x}_L)^2 = 25/10 = 2.5$; $s\bar{x}_H - \bar{x}_L = \sqrt{1.6 + 2.5} = \sqrt{4.1} = 2.02$ (c) $t = (25.6 - 20.2)/2.02 = 2.67$ (d) for $df = 18$, $t_{.05}$ (two-tailed) $= 2.10$; H_0 can be rejected at $\alpha = .05$ with bidirectional H_1; with unidirectional H_1 and one-tailed test, $t_{.01} = 2.55$, so H_0 can be rejected at .01. In either case, the investigator concludes that highly proficient individuals discriminate better than less proficient individuals.
(e) $\hat{\omega}_2 = \dfrac{(2.67)^2 + 1}{(2.67)^2 + 18 + 1} = 6.13/26.13 = .23$

V.   FURTHER EXERCISES

1.   Assume that data are available from two populations that turn out to have the same μ's and
σ's, as shown below. In both populations, the scores are normally distributed. Assume also
that an infinite number of pairs of random samples of 25 cases each were drawn from the
populations and the means ($\overline{X}_1$ and $\overline{X}_2$) determined for each pair.

$$\mu_1 = 95 \qquad \mu_2 = 95$$
$$\sigma_1 = 10 \qquad \sigma_2 = 10$$
$$\text{Sample N} = 25$$

(a)   What is the expected mean and standard deviation ($\sigma_{\overline{X}}$) of the sampling distribution of
$\overline{X}$'s from Population 1? Plot the sampling distribution of $\overline{X}$'s on the figure below,
recalling that for all practical purposes, all the $\overline{X}$'s will fall within the range
established by ±3 σ units. Indicate the mean and standard deviation ($\sigma_{\overline{X}}$) on your figure.
(Note that since μ's and σ's are the same, the sampling distribution for Population 2 is
identical to that for Population 1.)

$$\sigma_{\overline{X}_1} = \frac{10}{\sqrt{25}} = \frac{10}{5} = 2$$

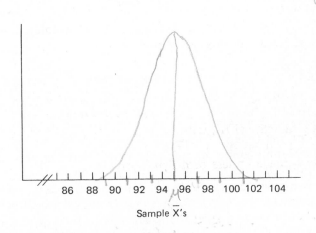

Sample $\overline{X}$'s

(b)   On the figure on the next page, plot the expected sampling distribution for the difference
between $\overline{X}$'s. In plotting the figure, first locate the mean of the distribution of
differences. Then, after considering the sampling distribution of $\overline{X}$'s for each population
(plotted in (a) above), estimate the approximate range, that is, the largest difference
($\overline{X}_1 - \overline{X}_2$) with a plus sign and with a minus sign that is expected. Having located the
mean and the upper and lower differences, sketch in the distribution. Finally, estimate
the value of the standard deviation ($\sigma_{\overline{X}_1 - \overline{X}_2}$) by inspection.

$$\sigma_{\overline{X}_1 - \overline{X}_2} = \sqrt{\sigma_{\overline{X}_1}^2 + \sigma_{\overline{X}_1}^2}$$
$$= \sqrt{\frac{\sigma_1^2}{N} + \frac{\sigma_2^2}{N}}$$
$$= \sqrt{\frac{100}{25} + \frac{100}{25}} = \sqrt{4+4} = \sqrt{8} = 2.8$$

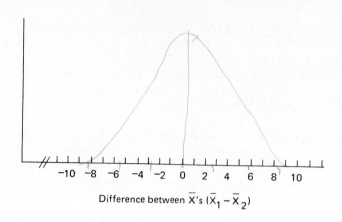

Difference between $\bar{X}$'s $(\bar{X}_1 - \bar{X}_2)$

(c) Comparison of the distributions in (a) and (b) should reveal that the sampling distribution of differences is more variable than either sampling distribution of $\bar{X}$'s. Why can this discrepancy in variability always be expected to occur? Relate this difference in variability to Formula 9.1 for $\sigma_{\bar{X}_1 - \bar{X}_2}$.

2. An investigator gave subjects a vigilance task requiring close attention under one of two conditions (20 subjects per group). The results showed that $\bar{X}_1 = 19.4$, $s_1 = 4.5$, and $\bar{X}_2 = 17.1$, $s_2 = 4.9$. Although the first condition produced better performance, as the investigator had predicted, t was only 1.55 and the null hypothesis could not be rejected. The investigator recalled that some construction work had been going on outside the laboratory, so the subjects were frequently distracted by noise. He decided to repeat the experiment, again with 20 subjects per group, this time in a quiet room. The results were $\bar{X}_1 = 20.7$, $s_1 = 3.7$, $\bar{X}_2 = 18.3$, $s_2 = 3.3$; t was 2.18 and H_0 was rejected at $\alpha = .05$. Another investigator replicated the experiment in all details, with 10 subjects per group. He found $\bar{X}_1 = 20.9$, $s_1 = 3.6$, $\bar{X}_2 = 18.4$, $s_2 = 3.4$, and $t = 1.59$.

   In each experiment, the difference between $\bar{X}$'s favored the original investigator's hypothesis but it was significant in only one instance. Which of the three experiments most likely led to the correct conclusion? Why?

3. An experimenter investigated whether the amount of prior information about an individual would be related to ease of memorizing new information about that individual. One group of 25 subjects was given the name of a well-known individual (e.g., Winston Churchill) and then a set of obscure facts about that individual (e.g., his favorite color) which they were asked to memorize. This procedure was repeated for a series of names. The second group of 25 was treated identically, except that the names they were given were fictitious (e.g., Alfred Black).

The following results were obtained, with the higher $\bar{X}$ indicating superior memorization.

Group 1	Group 2
(Well-known)	(Fictitious)
$\bar{X}_1 = 42.7$	$\bar{X}_2 = 37.3$
$s_1 = 5.6$	$s_2 = 5.8$

$$N = 25 \text{ per group} \qquad df = 50 - 2 = 48$$

(a) Compute $s_{\bar{X}_1 - \bar{X}_2}$.

$$s_{\bar{X}_1 - \bar{X}_2} = \sqrt{\frac{s_1^2}{N_1} + \frac{s_2^2}{N_2}} = \sqrt{\frac{31.36}{25} + \frac{33.64}{25}} = \sqrt{1.2544 + 1.3456}$$

$$= 1.61$$

Answer ___1.61___

(b) Draw an approximation of the sampling distribution of the difference between $\bar{X}$'s $(\bar{X}_1 - \bar{X}_2)$ that would be expected if $H_0: \mu_1 - \mu_2 = 0$ were true, using $s_{\bar{X}_1 - \bar{X}_2}$ as an estimate of $\sigma_{\bar{X}_1 - \bar{X}_2}$. On the baseline, label the score values $(\bar{X}_1 - \bar{X}_2)$ to be expected at the mean of the distribution, and at the points that are 1, 2, and 3 t-score units from the mean. Finally, locate the critical value of t at $\alpha = .01$ (two-tailed test).

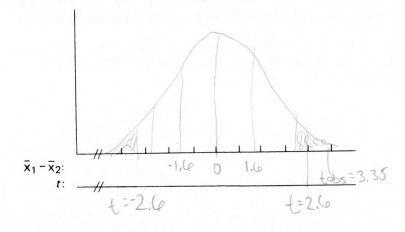

(c) Compute t and indicate where it falls in the hypothetical sampling distribution plotted in (b).

$$t = \frac{42.7 - 37.3}{1.61} = 3.35$$

Answer _____

(d) Assuming a bidirectional H_1, what do you conclude about H_0? Restate your conclusion in terms of the specific experiment.

Reject H_0

4. In a study of personal space, college students were individually brought into a waiting room, prior to a purported experiment, where a confederate of the investigator was already seated. The distance that the subject chose to sit from the confederate was observed. The investigator arranged to observe 15 students born and reared in the United States and 10 students born and reared in a mideastern country. The results for each group are shown below. (Higher numbers represent greater distance.)

Group 1	Group 2
United States	Mideastern
$\Sigma X = 315$	$\Sigma X = 180$
$\Sigma X^2 = 6785$	$\Sigma X^2 = 3368$
N $= 15$	N $= 10$

$\bar{X}_1 = \frac{315}{15} = 21$ $\bar{X}_2 = \frac{180}{10} = .18$

$s^2 = 12.14$

$s^2 = 14.22$

$$SS_1 = \Sigma X^2 - \frac{(\Sigma X)^2}{N}$$
$$= 6785 - \frac{(315)^2}{15}$$
$$= 170$$
$$S = \sqrt{\frac{170}{14}} = 3.48$$

$$SS = \Sigma X^2 + \frac{(\Sigma X)^2}{N}$$
$$= 3368 - \frac{(180)^2}{10}$$
$$= 128$$
$$S = \sqrt{\frac{128}{9}} = 3.77$$

106

What do you conclude about students from the two countries? In answering the question, specify the H_0 and H_1 you will test, the calculations entering into your computation of t, df, and the critical value of t at the α level you use. (Note that the N's in the two groups are not equal.) What is the estimated effect size?

a) $H_0: M_1 - M_2 = 0 \qquad H_1: M_1 - M_2 \neq 0$

b) $S_{\bar{X}_1 - \bar{X}_2} = \sqrt{\dfrac{(14)(12.14) + (9)(14.22)}{(15 + 10 - 2)} \left(\dfrac{1}{15} + \dfrac{1}{10}\right)}$

$= \sqrt{\dfrac{169.96 + 127.98}{23} \left(\dfrac{10}{150} + \dfrac{15}{150}\right)}$

$= \sqrt{(12.9539)(.16667)} \qquad = \sqrt{2.15898} = 1.469$

c) $t = \dfrac{(\bar{X}_1 - \bar{X}_2) - 0}{1.469} = \dfrac{3}{1.469} = 2.04$

d) $df = 23$

e) $t_{.05}(23) = 1.7139$

   Reject H_0

$n^2 = \dfrac{(2.04)^2}{(2.04^2 + 23)} = \dfrac{4.1616}{27.1616} = .1532$

$\hat{\omega}^2 = \dfrac{3.1616}{28.1616} = .1123$

$SS_{TOT} = 298$

$SS_{with} = 298$

Section M

Problems for Chapter 10:
Correlation

I. TERMS AND SYMBOLS TO REVIEW

Scatter plot

Linear correlation

Nonlinear correlation

Pearson product-moment
correlation coefficient (r)

z score cross-products

Coefficient of determination (r^2)

Coefficient of nondetermination ($1 - r^2$)

Standard error of estimate

Spearman rank-order correlation
coefficient (r_S)

Perfect correlation

II. SHORT-ANSWER QUESTIONS

1. The association between changes in one variable with changes in a second variable is
    identified as the _____ between variables.

2. When two variables are correlated, it cannot be assumed that changes in one variable
    _____ changes in the other.

3. In a scatter plot, each point represents _____
    _____.

4. When the line that comes closest to all the points in a scatter plot is a straight line, the
    correlation between the variables is (a) _____. When the line is curved, the
    correlation is (b) _____.

5. The Pearson product-moment correlation coefficient (r) is a measure of the amount of the
   (a) _____ between the variables. When all points lie along
   a straight line and high scores go with high scores, the correlation is called
   (b) _____ and r takes the value (c) _____. When
   all the points lie along a straight line and high scores go with low scores, the correlation is
   (d) _____ and r takes the value (e) _____. When there is
   no systematic change in one variable with changes in the other, r is equal to
   (f) _____.

6. Pearson r is defined as the mean of the _____.

7. In the computational formula for r, the expression ΣXY is found by _____
   _____.

8. The straight line that comes closest vertically to the data points in the columns of Y scores in
   a scatter plot is known as the (a) _____ or (b) _____ line of
   (c) _____ and is used to predict (d) _____ when only
   (e) _____ scores are known. Similarly, the straight line that comes closest
   horizontally to the data points in the column of X scores in a scatter plot is known as
   (f) _____ and is used to predict
   (g) _____.

9. Relative to each other, the positions of the two regression lines are (a) _____
   _____ when $r = 0$. When $r = \pm1.00$, they are (b) _____.
   Both regression lines always pass through the point that represents
   (c) _____.

10. The equation for a regression line takes the form of an equation for a (a) _____
    _____. The method that is used to determine regression lines is the
    (b) _____ method that keeps at a minimum (c) _____
    _____.

11. The coefficient of determination is equal to (a) _____ and indicates the
    proportion of the total variability among one set of scores that (b) _____
    _____.

12. The coefficient of nondetermination is equal to (a) _____ and indicates
    (b) _____
    _____.

13. The standard error of estimate for X and for Y represents the standard deviation of
    (a) _____. When $r = \pm1.00$, both
    standard errors of estimate are equal to (b) _____, indicating that there are

(c) _____ errors in prediction. When $r = 0$, the standard errors are equal to (d) _____.

14. The symbol r_S stands for the (a) _____ and represents (b) _____. Like r, the value of r_S ranges from (c) _____.

15. The H_0 almost always tested about the population r or r_S is that the population value is (a) _____. In evaluating this hypothesis for Pearson r, a special table is entered with $df =$ (b) _____. In evaluating this hypothesis for Spearman r, a special table is entered with (c) _____.

Answers

1. correlation   2. cause   3. the value of X and Y for a given pair of scores   4. (a) linear (b) nonlinear or curvilinear   5. (a) linear correlation or relationship   (b) perfect positive (c) +1.00   (d) perfect negative   (e) –1.00   (f) 0   6. z score cross-products   7. multiplying each X by the paired Y and summing the XY products   8. (a) and (b) regression, prediction (c) Y from X   (d) Y   (e) X   (f) the regression or prediction line of X from Y   (g) X when only Y is known   9. (a) at right angles, horizontal and vertical to the baseline   (b) identical   (c) X and Y   10. (a) straight line   (b) least squares   (c) the sum of the squares of the deviations of the points from the regression line   11. (a) r^2 (b) is explained by variations in the other set of scores   12. (a) $1 - r^2$ (b) the proportion of the total variability among one set of scores that is not explained by variations in the other set of scores   13. (a) the scores in a distribution around the regression line for any specific value of the predictor score   (b) 0   (c) no   (d) s_X and s_Y, the standard deviation of the X and Y distributions (or more precisely, the corrected estimate of the population standard deviation for each distribution)   14. (a) Spearman rank-order correlation coefficient   (b) the correlation or relationship between paired ranks   (c) +1.00 to –1.00   15. (a) 0   (b) N – 2   (c) N

III.   MULTIPLE-CHOICE QUESTIONS

_____ 1. Which of the following r values shows the strongest relationship between the X and Y variables?   (a) .65   (b) .22   (c) .00   (d) –.36   (e) –.72

_____ 2. People who earn high salaries tend to have larger vocabularies than people with low salaries. Causally, this means: (a) increasing vocabulary tends to increase salary   (b) increasing salary tends to increase vocabulary   (c) the correlation is due to some third variable, such as intelligence, that causes each   (d) no conclusion can be drawn from the correlation alone.

_____A_____ 3. Two scatter plots are shown below. The amount of correlation: (a) is higher in A than B   (b) is lower in A than B   (c) is about equal in A and B   (d) insufficient information is given to guess.

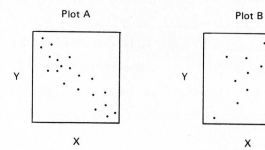

Plot A   Plot B

_____E_____ 4. When the linear correlation is perfect: (a) $r = \pm 1.00$ (b) there are no errors in predicting X from Y or Y from X   (c) the two regression lines are identical   (d) all the points in the scatter plot lie along a straight line   (e) all of the above are correct.

_____D_____ 5. When $r = 0$, the best estimate of Y from a known X is: (a) the standard deviation of X   (b) the standard deviation of Y   (c) $\bar{X}$ (d) $\bar{Y}$ (e) no prediction is possible.

_____C_____ 6. The r between two variables is .90. The percentage of the variability in Y scores accounted for by variability in X scores is: (a) 100%   (b) 90%   (c) 81%   (d) 50%   (e) can't tell from the information given.

_____A_____ 7. For the data shown in the scatter plot below, what is the most likely value of r?   (a) close to 0   (b) moderate positive   (c) high positive   (d) high negative   (e) moderate negative.

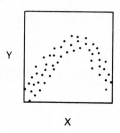

_____A_____ 8. Paired scores are converted to ranks and r_S is computed. The value of r_S, compared to r for the original raw scores, is: (a) similar to r (b) the same as r (c) the same as r only when there are no tied ranks   (d) greater than r (e) less than r.

Answers

1. (e)   2. (d)   3. (a)   4. (e)   5. (d)   6. (c)   7. (a)   8. (a)

IV. CALCULATIONAL PROBLEMS

1. Two measures have been obtained from each of 10 individuals, with the following results:

$$\Sigma X = 80 \qquad \Sigma Y = 60 \qquad \Sigma XY = 486$$
$$\Sigma X^2 = 636 \qquad \Sigma Y^2 = 369 \qquad N = 10$$
$$s_X = 1.33 \qquad s_Y = 1.00$$

(a) Find r.

Answer _____

(b) Test the hypothesis that the population r is 0.

Answer _____

(c) The regression equation for predicting Y from X is $Y_{pred} = .38X + 9.00$. Predict Y for X = 10.

Answer _____

(d) Find the regression equation for predicting X from Y.

Answer _____

(e) Find the coefficient of determination.

Answer _____

(f) Find $s_{\text{est } Y}$.

2. The X and Y scores obtained by 5 pairs of individuals are shown below. Convert each set of scores into ranks (highest score = 1).

Pair	X	R_X	Y	R_Y
1	21	_____	22	_____
2	21	_____	16	_____
3	30	_____	26	_____
4	19	_____	22	_____
5	23	_____	22	_____

3. For 10 pairs of ranks, the sum of the squared difference between each pair of ranks (Σd^2) is 220. Find r_S. Is it significant?

Answer _____

Answers

1. (a) By Formula 10.2, $r = \dfrac{486 - 10\,(8)\,(6)}{\sqrt{656 - 80^2/10}\ \sqrt{369 - 60^2/10}} = \dfrac{486 - 480}{\sqrt{16}\ \sqrt{9}} = \dfrac{6}{12} = .50$ (b) For $10 - 2 = 8\ df$, $r_{.05} = .632$. obtained r of .50 is not significant   (c) $Y_{\text{pred}} = .38\,(10) + 9 = 12.8$ (d) By Formula 10.6 $X_{\text{pred}} = [(.50)\,(1.33)/1.00]\,(Y) - [(.50)\,(1.33/1.00]\,(6) + 8 = .66(Y) - .66(6) + 8 = .66Y + 4.04$ (e) $r^2 = (.5)\,(.5) = .25$ (f) $s_{\text{est } Y} = 1.00\ \sqrt{1 - (.5)^2} = 1.00(.87) = .87$

2.

Pair	R_X	R_Y
1	3.5	3
2	3.5	5
3	1	1
4	5	3
5	2	3

3. By Formula 10.11, $r_S = 1 - \dfrac{6(220)}{10(100 - 1)} = 1 - (1320/990) = -.33$. For $N = 10$, r_S at .05 level is .648. Obtained r_S is not significant at $\alpha = .05$.

Name_____   Instructor_____

Date_____

V.   FURTHER EXERCISES

1.   Shown below are several sets of paired measures, expressed as z scores. Make a scatter plot for each set of data on the graphs below. Note that the graphs have been set up with four quadrants: pairs in which z_X and z_Y both lie above their means and therefore both have positive signs falling in the upper right quadrant, those in which both z's lie below their mean and therefore have negative signs falling in the lower left quadrant, etc. For each, describe the approximate magnitude of the correlation (high, medium, low, approximately zero) and the direction of the correlation. Include a reference to the distribution of the pairs among quadrants in coming to your conclusion about the correlation.

(a)

Pair	z_X	z_Y
1	−1.17	−2.06
2	.78	− .51
3	− .39	.38
4	1.56	1.52
5	− .78	− .04
6	1.17	1.00
7	.00	.06
8	.39	.65
9	−1.56	−1.09

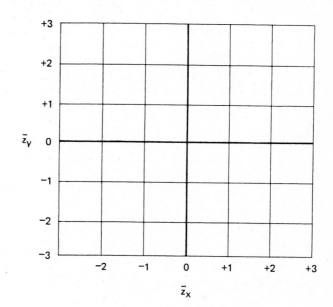

115

(b)

Pair	z_X	z_Y
1	− .19	.78
2	1.70	−1.61
3	− .19	− .47
4	.94	.47
5	.19	.16
6	−1.32	1.30
7	−1.70	1.09
8	1.32	− .78
9	− .94	− .16
10	.57	−1.20
11	.19	−1.41
12	− .57	−1.51

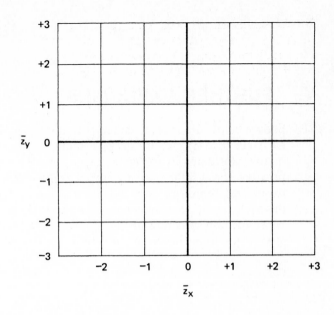

(c)

Pair	z_X	z_Y
1	.78	−1.00
2	.39	−2.00
3	1.56	.00
4	−1.17	− .50
5	− .78	−1.50
6	− .39	1.00
7	1.17	.60
8	−1.56	.40

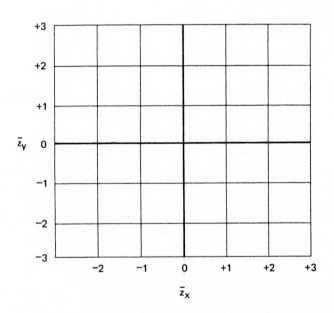

116

2. An investigator believes that individuals tend to be consistent in how careful or careless they are in performing routine tasks. He gives a group of 15 individuals a set of simple arithmetic problems to solve (X) and a second task in which they are given a prose passage and required to strike out the word "the" each time it occurs (Y). The numbers of errors made on the two tasks by the 15 individuals are shown below. Compute r. What do you conclude about consistency in performing routine tasks?

Ind.	Arith. (X)	Prose (Y)
1	3	2
2	4	5
3	3	5
4	4	4
5	1	2
6	5	3
7	1	2
8	5	7
9	7	6
10	10	10
11	0	1
12	8	9
13	2	4
14	11	13
15	4	6

$r =$ _____

Conclusion:

3. An instructor in a statistics class decides to correlate students' scores on the first midterm exam (X) with scores on the final (Y). A summary of the results is shown below.

$$\Sigma X = 700 \qquad \Sigma Y = 720$$
$$\Sigma X^2 = 25,000 \qquad \Sigma Y^2 = 26,640$$
$$N = 20 \qquad r = .60$$

(a) Find the regression equation for predicting final exam scores from midterm scores (Y from X).

(b) Predict the final exam scores for midterm scores of 26, 35, and 46.

X = 26 _____

X = 35 _____

X = 46 _____

(c) Find the regression equation for predicting X from Y.

Answer _____

(d) Plot the two regression lines on the figure below.

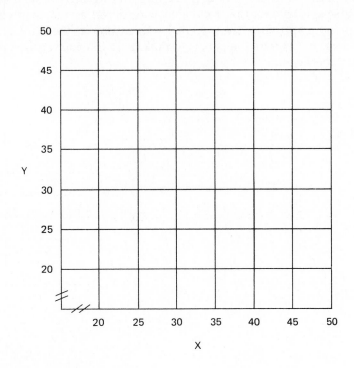

(e) What percentage of the variability in one set of exam scores is explained by variability in the other set of scores?

Answer _____

(f) Determine $s_{est\ Y}$.

Answer _____

(g) A student scored 31 on the midterm exam. After considering your answers to the questions above, how probable is it that he scored 37 or above on the final: Highly probable? Somewhat probable? Highly improbable? Explain.

119

4. An advertising executive suspects that men and women often react very differently to ads, a factor that should therefore be taken into account in planning promotional campaigns. He selects 8 different full-page layouts that are being considered as magazine ads for a new household product about to appear on the market. He then submits the 8 layouts to a panel of men and a panel of women and asks the panels to rank them in order of preference. Find the rank order correlation coefficient (r_S) for these data.

Ranks

Ad	Men	Women	
A	4	7	_____
B	1	4	_____
C	8	6	_____
D	3	1	_____
E	7	8	_____
F	6	2	_____
G	2	5	_____
H	5	3	_____

Answer _____

5. The grade average (on a 100-point scale) and the average amount of time per week spent watching TV are reported below for 6 high school students.

Student	Grade	TV
1	92	6
2	75	15
3	84	9
4	81	9
5	62	20
6	70	18

(a) Convert the scores to ranks and compute r_S.

Answer _____

120

(b) Can it be concluded that in these students, too much time watching TV causes poor grades? Explain.

Section N

Problems for Chapter 11:
Sampling Distributions: Matched Pairs

I.   TERMS AND SYMBOLS TO REVIEW

Matched pairs   Standard error of mean difference ($s_{\bar{D}}$)

Direct difference method df for matched pairs

Mean difference ($\bar{D}$)   Sandler's A statistic

II.   SHORT-ANSWER QUESTIONS

1. In an experiment employing two conditions, it is sometimes feasible to test each subject under each condition, thus producing (a) _____ of scores. A similar procedure is to select pairs of different individuals who (b) _____

    _____.

2. The use of matched pairs in an experiment has the potential advantage of increasing the power of a t test to (a) _____ by reducing the value of (b) _____ and thus increasing the value of

    (c) _____.

3. When the correlation between pairs of scores on the dependent measure is taken into account in computing t and r is positive, the value of $s_{\bar{x}_1 - \bar{x}_2}$ (a) _____ and the value of t

(b) _____. When the correlation is 0, the values of $s_{\bar{X}_1 - \bar{X}_2}$ and t are

(c) _____ as would be obtained by computing a random groups t.

4. The df for a matched groups t is equal to (a) _____ where N is

(b) _____; for a random groups t, df is equal to

(c) _____.

5. The basic data entering into the direct difference method for computing t are

(a) _____ of raw scores. The H_0 that

is tested about the mean difference ($\bar{D}$) in the population is that (b) _____.

In the direct difference method, the equivalent of $s_{\bar{X}_1 - \bar{X}_2}$ (which includes r) is symbolized as

(c) _____.

6. A second short method of testing the hypothesis that $\mu_1 - \mu_2 = 0$ for matched pairs is

(a) _____ that is also based on (b) _____ scores.

The smaller the value of this statistic, the (c) _____ significant it is.

Answers

1. (a) matched pairs   (b) are matched in one or more relevant characteristics   2. (a) detect a
false H_0 (b) $s_{\bar{X}_1 - \bar{X}_2}$ (c) t 3. (a) decreases   (b) increases   (c) the same   4.
(a) N − 1   (b) number of pairs of scores   (c) $N_1 + N_2 - 2$ 5. (a) the differences (D) between
pairs (of X's)   (b) $\bar{D} = 0$ (c) $s_{\bar{D}}$ 6. (a) Sandler's A statistic   (b) difference   (c) more

III. CALCULATIONAL PROBLEMS

1. The following data have been obtained in an experiment employing 20 matched pairs of subjects.

$$\bar{X}_1 = 130 \qquad\qquad \bar{X}_2 = 120$$

$$s_{\bar{X}_1} = 3 \qquad\qquad s_{\bar{X}_2} = 4$$

$$N = 20 \qquad\qquad r_{12} = .50$$

(a) Compute a random groups t. Using $\alpha = .05$ and a two-tailed test, what do you conclude about H_0?

(b)   Compute a matched groups t. Using $\alpha = .05$ and a two-tailed test, what do you conclude about H_0? If your conclusion differs from (a), which is more likely to be correct?

2.   In an experiment involving 10 matched pairs, the difference (D) was found between each pair of scores, with the following results:

$$\Sigma D = 30 \qquad \Sigma D^2 = 205 \qquad N = 10$$

(a)   Test H_0 by computing a direct difference t. What do you conclude?

(b)   Test H_0 by computing Sandler's A. What do you conclude? Check to see that your conclusion is the same as in (a).

Answers

1. (a) $s_{\bar{x}_1 - \bar{x}_2} = \sqrt{3^2 + 4^2} = 5$; $t = (130 - 120)/5 = 2.00$; with $df = 38$, $t_{.05} = 2.03$. H_0 cannot be rejected
(b) $s_{\bar{x}_1 - \bar{x}} = \sqrt{3^2 + 4^2 - 2(.50)\,(3)\,(4)} = 3.61$; $t = 10/3.61 = 2.77$, with $df = 19$, $t_{.05} = 2.09$; H_0 is rejected at 5% level. The matched groups t has more power, reducing the probability of a Type II error without increasing the probability of a Type I error.   2. (a) $\bar{D} = 3.00$; $s_D^2 = [205 - (30/10)]/(10 - 1) = 12.78$; $s_{\bar{D}} = \sqrt{12.78/10} = 1.13$; $t = 3/1.13 = 2.65$. With $df = 9$, $t_{.05} = 2.26$; H_0 is rejected at 5% level.   (b) $A = 205/(30)^2 = .228$; with $df = 9$, maximum A for $\alpha = .05$ (two-tailed test) is .276; H_0 is rejected at 5% level, as in (a).

IV.   FURTHER EXERCISES

1. A social psychologist wanted to determine whether high school students were more or less liberal in their political attitudes than their same-sex parent, as measured by scores on an objective questionnaire. The results below are from a group of 36 girls (X) and their mothers (Y). Higher scores indicate greater liberality.

$\Sigma X = 918$ $\Sigma Y = 774$ $\Sigma X^2 = 24{,}468$ $\Sigma Y^2 = 17{,}516$ $\Sigma XY = 20{,}133$

$\bar{X} = 25.5$ $\bar{Y} = 21.5$

(a)   Do mothers and daughters differ significantly?

(b)   Whether or not the means differ significantly determine whether there is a significant resemblance between mothers and their daughters in their attitudes.

2. Individuals seeking cosmetic facial surgery (for a very prominent or deformed nose, receding chin, and so forth) often suffer from low self-confidence and self-esteem. To determine whether surgery improves self-concept, a study was conducted in which 12 patients were given a battery of psychological tests preoperatively and were retested one year postoperatively. The results for one test are shown below (with high scores indicating greater self-esteem).

Patient	Pre	Post
1	31	34
2	26	25
3	32	38
4	38	36
5	29	29
6	34	41
7	24	26
8	35	42
9	30	36
10	36	44
11	31	28
12	27	32

(a) Using the direct difference method to compute t, determine whether there was a significant *increase* in self-esteem following surgery. (Test H_1: $\mu_{Pre} < \mu_{Post}$, using a one-tailed test.)

(b) Test the same H_0 and H_1 by Sandler's A statistic.

Special Review:

Summary of Hypothesis Testing: Determination of the Appropriate Statistical Test

This Special Review has two purposes. The first is to summarize the steps we must go through to test the kinds of null hypotheses that have been discussed to this point in the textbook, and to demonstrate the parallel logic that is used for testing each of these H_0's. This summary is found in the section immediately below.

The second purpose is to discuss the kind of reasoning we use in deciding what statistical test to conduct with the data from a research study to answer the question posed by the investigator. Research questions do not come with prepackaged research designs and plans for data analyses. These must be devised by the investigator. Although the broad topic of research design is beyond the purview of this course, it is possible to give you practice in examining particular studies and determining the most appropriate statistical test to use.

In Chapter 16 of the textbook you will find a "decision tree" which outlines the series of decisions to make about a given set of data that will allow you to determine what statistic to compute or what statistical test to conduct. This decision tree, which incorporates all the statistical tests presented in the text, is reproduced in Section U of this *Workbook*. In this Special Review, we introduce you to those portions of the decision tree that are relevant to the techniques that are covered through Chapter 11 of the text and give you practice in using the decision tree to identify the appropriate test for specific sets of data.

Steps in Testing Null Hypotheses

In Chapters 8 through 11 of the textbook we discussed techniques for testing several kinds of null hypotheses. Testing each of these particular H_0's requires us to convert our obtained sample statistic into a z score or a t (estimated z) score that is based on the assumption that the value of the population parameter specified in H_0 is correct. One of these tests involves categorical data, more specifically, the binomial situation in which there is a set of two mutually exclusive categories and the hypothesis is that in the population, a specified proportion of cases falls into the favored category (p). All the rest of the tests involve numerical data.

Table 1

Steps in Testing H_0 and Bidirectional H_1 for Various Population Parameters

STEPS	NUMERICAL DATA				
	Single Sample	*Two Independent Samples*	*Matched Pairs*		
			Difference Between Groups	Correlation	
				r	r_S
1. Set up H_0 and H_1 for pop. parameter H_0 H_1	μ = (specific value) $\mu \neq$ (value in H_0)	$\mu_1 - \mu_2 = 0$ $\mu_1 - \mu_2 \neq 0$	$\mu_1 - \mu_2 = 0$ $\mu_1 - \mu_2 \neq 0$	$r=0$ $r\neq0$	$r_S=0$ $r_S\neq0$
2. Test sample(s); find statistic parallel to pop. parameter in H_0	$\bar{X}$	$\bar{X}_1 - \bar{X}_2$	$\bar{X}_1 - \bar{X}_2$ or $\bar{X}_D$	r	r_S
3. Convert statistic to t or z assuming H_0				(Not necessary to determine)	
(a) Find standard error	$s_{\bar{X}} = s/\sqrt{N}$	$s_{\bar{X}_1 - \bar{X}_2} =$ $\sqrt{s_{\bar{X}_1}^2 + s_{\bar{X}_2}^2}$ (equal N's) where $s_{\bar{X}} = s/\sqrt{N}$	By direct difference method: $s_{\bar{D}} =$ $\sqrt{\dfrac{s_D^2}{N}}$		
(b) Find t or z	$t = \dfrac{\bar{X}-\mu}{s_{\bar{X}}}$	$t = \dfrac{(\bar{X}_1 - \bar{X}_2)}{s_{\bar{X}_1 - \bar{X}_2}}$	$t = \dfrac{\bar{X}_D}{s_{\bar{D}}}$		
4. Find df	$df = N-1$	$df = N_1 + N_2 - 2$	$df=$ N–1 where N= no. of pairs	$df=$ N–2 where N= no. of pairs	N
5. Find critical value of t, z or r at $\alpha_{.05}$ or $\alpha_{.01}$ for df	t table (Table C)	t table (Table C)	t table (Table C)	r table (Table D)	r_S table (Table E)
6. Evaluate H_0	Reject H_0 if calculated t, z or r exceeds critical value at the given α level.				

The tests we have discussed are summarized in Table 1. The type of data, numerical or categorical, is shown at the top of the table and then, under these headings, sample characteristics are indicated. The step-by-step procedures that are taken to test the kinds of H_0's we have discussed are listed at the left of the table. In each case, we first set up a null hypothesis (H_0) and an alternative hypothesis (H_1) about the population parameter of interest. (For simplicity of presentation, we have set up only a bidirectional H_1.) We then test a sample (or pair of samples) and from the sample data determine the statistic that is parallel to the population parameter. Next (except for r and r_s), we convert this sample statistic into a t or z score, which requires that we calculate the standard error of the hypothetical sampling distribution of the given population parameter whose mean takes the value specified in H_0. Then, when called for, we determine df.

Finally, we determine from the appropriate table the critical value of t, z or r at $\alpha = .05$ or $\alpha = .01$ and by comparing the critical value with our obtained value of t or z, we reach a decision about whether to reject H_0 at our chosen α level or not to reject it.

By examining Table 1 you should be able to discern the common statistical logic that underlies all of these tests. Once you grasp the similarities among the different kinds of tests you should be able to understand more clearly the process of testing hypotheses about population parameters.

Decision Tree

The full decision tree, we remind you, is shown in Section U of this *Workbook* and also in Chapter 16 of the text. In this decision tree, a series of decisions must be made, with the outcome of each decision leading to the next decision, ultimately culminating in identification of the appropriate statistical test. We have enclosed each of these decisions within a diamond and have enclosed the outcome of each decision within a box. We will go over here only those portions of the decision tree that are relevant to the techniques discussed through Chapter 11.

The initial decision that must be made involves a determination of the type of data that has been obtained. Thus:

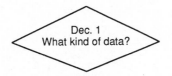

The question asks what kind of information has been collected from the individual case in the sample or series of samples. There are two major possibilities: (1) the individual has been assigned to one of two or more mutually exclusive *categories* (e.g., male or female; yes, no, or maybe), or (2) the individual has been assigned a number (or occasionally, a rank indicating relative position in a group) that reflects *how much* of a property the individual exhibits (e.g., length in millimeters, time in seconds, number of correct responses). In the first instance, locate the IF CATEGORICAL box in the decision tree and proceed to the next decision; in the second instance, locate the IF NUMERICAL box and proceed.

IF CATEGORICAL

Only one statistical test involving categorical data has thus far been presented: a test of a hypothesis about a population proportion (p) from a binomial situation in which each individual case is assigned to one of two mutually exclusive categories. The hypothesis to be tested about the population p is either directly stated or is implied in the description of the investigator's purpose in conducting the study. The test involves computation of a z score, using Formula 8.9.

In later chapters, techniques will be presented for analyzing data in which two or more categories are involved.

IF NUMERICAL

If the property exhibited by the individual case exists along a dimension, a second decision must be made.

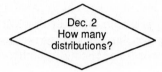

Locate the appropriate number of distributions (IF statement) and proceed.

IF ONE

If only one distribution of measures has been obtained, a question is being asked about a single population. Only questions about the population μ have been discussed in the text, which leads to the third decision.

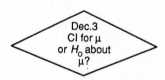

The third decision is: Is a hypothesis to be tested about the value of μ or is a confidence interval (CI) for μ to be obtained?

(a) Problems asking for a CI to be set up either specify so directly or inquire about a range of values within which (at a given confidence level) it can be asserted that μ falls. Use Formula 8.6 or 8.7.

(b) In problems calling for a test of a hypothesis about μ, the value of μ in H_0 is either stated directly or is implied in the statement of the problem. A t is computed using Formula 8.4.

IF TWO

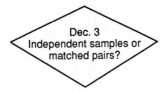

Dec. 3
Independent samples or
matched pairs?

When there are two distributions (samples), the third decision is: Do the two distributions (samples) of measures represent two independently selected samples or do they represent matched pairs?

IF INDEPENDENT

Only a technique for testing a hypothesis about the difference between population μ's has been presented in the text. The H_0 that is conventionally tested is that $\mu_1 - \mu_2 = 0$. A random groups t is computed, using Formula 9.5.

IF MATCHED PAIRS

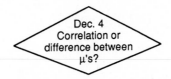

Dec. 4
Correlation or
difference between
μ's?

The techniques presented in the text allow only two possibilities.

(a) A question is being asked about the *correlation* between the matched pairs of measures. Key words suggesting that calculation of a correlation coefficient is called for are relationship, association, covariation, or resemblance.

When the original data are reported in ranks, the Spearman r_S should be computed by Formula 10.11. When the individual case is assigned a number indicating how much of the property is exhibited, a Pearson r can be computed (by Formula 10.2) from the two distributions of numbers or the data can be converted into ranks and r_S computed.

If interest is in the population correlation, the H_0 that is typically tested, based on sample data, is that r or r_S equals 0.

(b) A question is instead being asked about the difference between μ's with H_0 conventionally being that $\mu_1 - \mu_2 = 0$. Compute a matched groups t by the direct difference method (see Formula 11.5) or compute Sandler's A statistic (see Formula 11.6).

133

Techniques for analyzing measurement data in which two or more independent groups are to be compared are presented in Chapters 12 and 13 of the text. Application of the decision tree to these data will be discussed in a later Special Review.

Examples

With these explanations before us we can now consider several concrete examples to demonstrate how to use the decision tree. Listed below the description of the study is the answer to each decision.

1. Members of a sample of married couples are given a test measuring attitudes about child-rearing practices, with low scores indicating highly permissive beliefs and high scores indicating rule-oriented beliefs. Do husbands and wives resemble each other in their attitudes?

Decision 1. Numerical data.

Decision 2. There are two distributions of measures, one for husbands and one for wives.

Decision 3. The two distributions represent matched pairs (wife and husband).

Decision 4. The question asks about husband-wife *resemblance*, calling for the computation of a correlation coefficient. Since each individual has been assigned a number, Pearson r is appropriate. The hypothesis to be tested is that in the population, $r = 0$.

2. In a study of guessing biases in 5-year-old children, the experimenter holds out two fists and asks each child to guess in which hand he has hidden a penny. Each child's choice of right or left is recorded.

Decision 1. Categorical data.

Decision 2. One set of categories (the set is right or left).

Decision 3. The number of categories is two.

The research question calls for a test of a hypothesis about the population proportion (p) in the favored category (which we will arbitrarily say is "right"; the proportion in the nonfavored category, "left," is designated as q). If there is no guessing bias, then the split between categories is equal ($p = .50$, $q = .50$); if there is a bias, the split is unequal. Since H_0 calls for an exact value, the null hypothesis to be tested (by computing z) is that $p = .50$; H_1 is that $p \neq .50$.

3. Studies by gerontologists have shown that memory for new information tends to be impaired in elderly people. A brain chemical has recently been identified that has promise for reducing this impairment. Randomly selected residents of a retirement home are given the chemical for a month, and then are given a memory task. A second randomly selected group of residents, given an inert substance in place of the experimental chemical, serves as a control group. For both groups, the dependent measure is number of trials to perfect recall of the material to be memorized.

Decision 1. Numerical data.

Decision 2. Two distributions of measures.

Decision 3. Two independently selected samples.

The research question asks whether or not the chemical had an effect on memory; that is, whether or not the two samples came from populations with the same μ's with respect to performance on the memory task. Compute a random groups t, testing $H_0: \mu_1 - \mu_2 = 0$ and either a bidirectional $H_1 (\mu_1 - \mu_2) \neq 0$, or a unidirectional $H_1 (\mu_1 - \mu_2 > 0)$ predicting that the experimental group is superior.

4. In an investigation of sex stereotypes in which female high school students served as subjects, one item inquired about men vs. women drivers. Subjects answered on a 5-point scale, 5 indicating that men are much better drivers than women, 3 indicating that the sexes are equal, and 1 that women are much better than men. Is there a stereotype?

Decision 1. Numerical data.

Decision 2. One distribution of scores.

Decision 3. The question calls for a t test of a hypothesis about μ.

If there is no stereotype about sex differences in driving among female high school students, then $\mu = 3$, that is, the point on the rating scale indicating that men and women are equal. If there is a stereotype, $\mu \neq 3$. Since a null hypothesis must specify an exact value, $H_0: \mu = 3$. In case there is a sex stereotype, the investigator has not specified in advance whether females are biased in favor of their own sex or in favor of males. Therefore, only a bidirectional H_1 can be set up ($\mu \neq 3$).

Practice Problems

For each of the following examples, determine the statistic to be computed or the statistical test to be conducted. Indicate your answer by choosing the appropriate test from the following list. Then specify H_0 and H_1 (if applicable).

(a) z for population p (b) confidence interval for μ (c) t test of hypothesis about μ (d) random groups t test of hypothesis about differences between μ's   (e) matched pairs t test of hypothesis about difference between μ's   (f) Pearson r (g) Spearman r_S

1. Male subjects were shown pairs of slides of faces showing various emotions (happy, sad, angry, fearful). Sometimes the emotions in a pair were the same and sometimes they were different. Each pair of slides was briefly exposed, the subjects' task being to identify whether the pair was the same or different. One member of each pair was exposed at the center of a screen. Half the time the second member of the pair appeared at the right of the screen and half the time it appeared at the left. For each subject, the number of correct identifications was obtained for pairs in which one member appeared on the right and for pairs in which one member appeared on the left. The experimenter was interested in whether processing of information about facial expressions differed according to whether the information was presented in the right or left visual field.

Test _____

H_0 _____ H_1 _____

2. Undergraduate students majoring in business or in psychology were asked to order a series of 10 life values (money, leisure, prestige, helping others, etc.) according to their personal importance. For each group of students, the mean rating of each life value was obtained, the value with the highest mean being assigned a rank of 1, the second highest a rank of 2, etc. Are business and psychology students similar in their values?

Test _____

H_0 _____ H_1 _____

3. A group of 20 young laboratory animals was fed each day a food mixture whose flavor was made distinctive by addition of peppermint extract. After 3 months on this regimen, each animal was given a choice on 10 successive days of eating from a dish containing the usual mixture or from a dish in which the food had a licorice flavor but was otherwise identical. (Prior studies showed that the two flavors were equally palatable.) The investigator was interested in determining whether familiarity with incidental cues, such as flavor, had long-term effects on food preferences. The data that were analyzed were choices on day 10. It was found that 17 of the animals selected the familiar flavor and 3 the different flavor.

Test _____

H_0 _____ H_1 _____

4. In an investigation comparing a group of delinquent boys and a group of nondelinquent boys, each boy was given a test measuring the tendency to blame his failures or inadequacies on other people and to deny any personal responsibility. Scores on this test had a possible range of 1 to 30.

Test _____

H_0 _____ H_1 _____

5. In a laboratory study of self-disclosure, women subjects were seen by a female interviewer who asked them to talk on the topic "things that bother me" for 10 minutes. The tapes of their responses were later rated for overall intimacy of self-disclosure (e.g., a woman who talked about being bothered by her roommate's poor housekeeping and similar things received a lower intimacy score than a woman who discussed her disagreements with her parents or her inability to make friends). Scores were available for these women on a test of extroversion, the investigator being interested in determining whether degree of extroversion is related to intimacy of self-disclosure.

Test _____

H_0 _____ H_1 _____

136

6. As part of a battery of physical fitness tests, members of a sample of 10-year-old boys are asked to hold their breath as long as possible; $\overline{X}$ is 38 seconds. Within what range of values can it be asserted that μ falls?

Test _____

H_0 _____ H_1 _____

7. A nationally administered test of math achievement in elementary school students is scored such that the average (standardized) score at any given grade level is 100. A psychologist interested in the possibility that divorce has short-term adverse effects on children's achievement obtains the scores of a group of children whose parents have been divorced within the previous year.

Test _____

H_0 _____ H_1 _____

Answers

1. (e); H_0: $\mu_R - \mu_L = 0$; H_1: $\mu_R - \mu_L \neq 0$ 2. (g); H_0: $r_S = 0$; H_1: $r_S \neq 0$ 3. (a); H_0: pop $p = .50$; H_1: pop $p \neq .50$ 4. (d); H_0: $\mu_D - \mu_{ND} = 0$; H_1: $\mu_D - \mu_{ND} \neq 0$ 5. (f); H_0: $r = 0$; H_1: $r \neq 0$ 6. (b); H_0 and H_1: none   7. (c); H_0: $\mu = 100$; H_1: $\mu \neq 100$ or $\mu < 100$

Section P

Problems for Chapter 12:
One-Way Analysis of Variance

I. TERMS TO REVIEW

Total variability	Sum of squares between groups (SS_{bg})
Variability within groups	Mean square within groups (MS_{wg})
Variability between groups	Mean square between groups (MS_{bg})
Total sum of squares (SS_{tot})	F ratio
Sum of squares within groups (SS_{wg})	Tukey honestly significant difference
	(hsd) test

II. SHORT-ANSWER QUESTIONS

1. Analysis of variance, which is often identified by the acronym (a) _____, is a technique used to compare the means of (b) _____ groups. When applied to the results of investigations in which the effects of only one type of independent variable are being studied, the technique is identified as (c) _____ analysis of variance.

2. The basic fact underlying ANOVA is that the total variability among the pooled scores from all the subjects in an experiment can be assigned to two categories or sources: variability of scores (a) _____ and variability (b) _____.

3. The null hypothesis that is tested by the one-way ANOVA technique is that
(a) _____. This H_0 is tested by finding two variances, the variance
(b) _____ and the variance (c) _____. If H_0 is correct, the
variance (d) _____ is expected to be small in comparison to the variance
(e) _____.

4. The first step in conducting an ANOVA is to determine the sum of squares for
(a) _____, abbreviated as (b) _____. This quantity represents the sum of
(c) _____
_____.
This sum of squares is divided into two components. The first is the sum of squares within
groups, abbreviated as (d) _____. This quantity represents the sum of (e) _____
_____.
The second component is (f) _____, which represents the sum of
(g) _____.

5. The next step in conducting ANOVA is to determine the within-group variance and the
between-group variance. Each of these variances is also called a (a) _____.
SS_{wg} and SS_{bg} are the (b) _____ in the formulas for these variances. The
denominators in the variance formulas are (c) _____.

6. The df_{tot} is equal to (a) _____, df_{wg} is equal to (b) _____, and df_{bg} is equal
to (c) _____. The sum of df_{wg} and df_{bg} equals (d) _____.

7. Dividing MS_{bg} by MS_{wg} produces the _____.

8. F is interpreted by locating in the F table the critical value of F for the given α level
associated with (a) _____. If the calculated value of F is larger
than the critical value, H_0 is (b) _____ and it is concluded that the population μ's
(c) _____.

9. It is appropriate to conduct ANOVA if three assumptions are met. These are that each of the
populations from which the samples were drawn is (a) _____, that the
(b) _____ of the populations are equal, and that each sample
(c) _____.

10. A (a) _____ following ANOVA is used to determine the
significance of the difference between specific pars or pairs of subsets of means. One such test,
discussed in the text, is (b) _____. In this
test, a quantity identified as (c) _____ is calculated which indicates (d) _____
_____ that must be obtained for the
difference to be significant at a given α level.

11. An estimate of the proportion of the variability in the dependent variable that can be accounted for by variations in the independent variable is given by _____.

Answers

1. (a) ANOVA   (b) two or more groups   (c) one-way   2. (a) within each group
(b) between the groups   3. (a) the means of the populations from which the samples were drawn are equal   (b) between groups   (c) within groups   (d) between groups   (e) within groups   4. (a) total   (b) SS_{tot} (c) the squared deviations of each of the scores from the overall grand mean for the combined groups   (d) SS_{wg} (e) the squared deviations of each score from the mean of its own group   (f) sum of squares between groups (SS_{bg})   (g) the squared deviations of each group mean from the overall grand mean   5. (a) mean square (MS)
(b) numerators   (c) the number of degrees of freedom within groups and between groups (df_{wg} and df_{bg})   6. (a) $N_{tot} - 1$ (b) $N_{tot} - k$, where k equals the number of groups   (c) $k - 1$ (d) df_{tot}
7. F ratio   8. (a) df_{bg} and df_{wg} (df's associated with the numerator and denominator of the F ratio)   (b) rejected   (c) are not all equal   9. (a) normally distributed   (b) variances (σ^2's)
(c) was randomly and independently selected from its parent population   10. (a) multiple comparison test   (b) Tukey's honestly significant difference test   (c) hsd (d) the minimal difference between any given pair of $\bar{X}$'s   11. $\hat{\omega}^2$

III.   CALCULATIONAL PROBLEMS

The following data were computed from the results of a three-group experiment in which there were 20 subjects per group.

$$\bar{X}_1 = 19.2 \qquad \bar{X}_2 = 20.6 \qquad \bar{X}_3 = 16.9$$
$$SS_{tot} = 399 \qquad SS_{bg} = 57 \qquad SS_{wg} = 342$$

1. What is H_0?

2. Fill in the remaining values in the summary table shown below.

Source	SS	df	MS	F
Between groups	57	____	____	____
Within groups	342	____	____	
Total	399	____		

3. For df's of (a) _____, $F_{.05}$ = (b) _____ and $F_{.01}$ = (c) _____ . The obtained F is (d) _____ at the (e) _____ level and H_0 is (f) _____ .

141

4. (a) Compute *hsd*, using $\alpha = .05$.
   (b) Determine at $\alpha = .05$ which pairs of $\bar{X}$'s differ significantly from each other.

5. Compute $\hat{\omega}^2$. What do you conclude about effect size?

Answers

1. The population means are all equal ($\mu_1 = \mu_2 = \mu_3$).

2.

Source	SS	df	MS	F
Between groups	57	2	28.5	4.75
Within groups	342	57	6.0	
Total	399	59		

3. (a) 2 and 57   (b) 3.23   (c) 5.18   (d) significant   (e) 5%   (f) rejected
4. (a) $hsd = 3.44 \sqrt{6/20} = 3.44(.55) = 1.89$ (b) $\bar{X}_1$ and $\bar{X}_2$ differ less than 1.89 and thus do not differ significantly. However, both $\bar{X}_1$ and $\bar{X}_2$ differ significantly at the 5% level from $\bar{X}_3$.
5. $\hat{\omega}^2 = \dfrac{57 - (3-1)(6)}{399 + 6} = \dfrac{45}{405} = .11$. The independent variable had a moderate effect.

IV.   FURTHER EXERCISES

1.   Individuals who complain that they have difficulty sticking up for their rights and expressing opinions and desires are often given "assertiveness training." At a Student Counseling Center, a counselor decided to compare the effectiveness of several methods of training. He identified 40 nonassertive males who were seeking help and assigned them randomly to one of four groups. In Group 1, a group discussion procedure was used in which the students talked about their problem and discussed how they might overcome it (Group Discussion condition). In Group 2, students were presented with a series of imaginary situations in which assertive behavior was appropriate and required to rehearse what they should say and do (Rehearsal condition). In Group 3, students not only had this behavioral practice, but also observed a model reacting to the situations in a competent, assured manner (Rehearsal Plus Modeling). Members of Group 4 were informed that they could not be accommodated in a treatment group for another month (Control condition). All treatments were conducted over the month period. At the end of this time, all students were asked to role-play their reactions to several individuals whose script called for them to be demanding and to put pressure on the students to do something they didn't want to do. The assertiveness exhibited by each student in resisting these demands was assessed by a panel of trained judges, high scores indicating more assertiveness. A summary of the results is shown below.

$$\Sigma X_1 = 56 \qquad \Sigma X_2 = 100 \qquad \Sigma X_3 = 124 \qquad \Sigma X_4 = 50$$
$$\Sigma X_1^2 = 316 \qquad \Sigma X_2^2 = 1084 \qquad \Sigma X_3^2 = 1644 \qquad \Sigma X_4^2 = 288$$
$$N = 10 \text{ per group}$$

(a)   What is the null hypothesis of the study? (Be concrete in referring to the specific study being conducted.)

(b)   Perform an ANOVA of the data, summarizing the results in the following source table.

Source	SS	df	MS	F
Between groups	____	____	____	____
Within groups	____	____	____	
Total	____	____	____	

(c)   State your conclusion about the significance of F and H_0.

(d)   Graph the results.

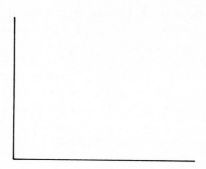

(e)   After inspecting the graph of the means and the results of your analysis, describe the outcome of the study.

(f)   To check your informal impressions in (e), perform the *hsd* test. What do you conclude?

2.   A social psychologist interested in self-fulfilling prophecies conducted an experiment in which college students were asked to interview a female student in her Freshman year on the general topic of how she was adjusting to college life. (In each pair, the persons were in a different room and communicated by telephone.) One third of the students were told that a previously administered personality test indicated that the young woman they would interview was a quite anxious, depressed person. Another third were told that the test indicated that she was happy and self-confident. The remaining third of the students were given no information. (In actuality, all the women scored in the middle range on the personality test.) After the experiment, raters who were blind to the experimental conditions listened to tape recordings of the women's responses and made a judgment about how confident and well adjusted each woman was. The results are shown below, with *low* scores indicating better adjustment. The investigator hypothesized that the interviewers' expectations about the woman they interviewed would influence how they interviewed her in a way that would produce the kind of behavior they expected.

Control	Happy	Depressed
9	7	15
6	3	12
8	5	19
7	10	14
10	8	17

(a) Perform an ANOVA of these data. What do you conclude about H_0?

(b) After inspecting the means of the groups and your ANOVA, what conclusions do you draw about the effects of the interviewer's expectations about the woman he is interviewing on the woman's responses?

(c) What is your estimate of effect size?

3. Shown below are the scores received in a three group experiment. Do any of the assumptions of ANOVA appear to be violated? If so, what?

Group 1	Group 2	Group 3
10	7	3
10	9	5
11	10	9
11	11	15
12	11	18
14	12	20
17	13	22
19	15	25
22	16	31

● **Section Q**

Problems for Chapter 13:
Two-Way Analysis of Variance

● ## I.   TERMS AND SYMBOLS TO REVIEW

Two-way factorial design   A X B interaction

Main effects H_0 for A X B interaction

H_0 for main effects   Additive interaction

II.   SHORT-ANSWER QUESTIONS

1. Experiments in which the effects of variations in two types of independent variables are simultaneously studied employ what is called a two-way (a) _____ design. If there were 3 conditions within variable A and 2 conditions within variable B, the design would call for (b) _____ X _____ groups, for a total of (c) _____.

2. Analysis of the data from a two-way factorial design by means of a

(a) _____ ANOVA permits the test of three null hypotheses. The first H_0 is about the (b) _____ of variable A. This hypothesis states that

(c) _____

_____

_____.

● The second H_0 is about (d) _____ and states that

(e) _____

_____

_____.

The third H_0 is about the (f) _____ of variables A and B and states that

(g) _____

_____

_____.

3. In computing a two-way ANOVA, the first step is to determine the sum of squares (SS) for

    (a) _____. This SS is then broken down into two components: (b) _____ and

    _____, using the same techniques as in (c) _____ ANOVA. The sum of

    squares (d) _____ is, in turn, broken down into three components:

    (e) _____, _____, and _____. Of these three, the SS's for

    (f) _____ are computed directly from the raw scores. The SS for

    (g) _____ is typically obtained by subtraction, using the formula

    (h) _____.

4. The df associated with variable A is equal to (a) _____; for variable B, df is equal

    to (b) _____, and for the A X B interaction, df is equal to (c) _____.

    The sum of these df's is equal to the (d) _____ df. The df within groups is equal to

    (e) _____. The sum of the df's for (f) _____ is equal to df_{tot}.

5. After determining each SS and its associated df, four (a) _____ or variances

    are computed. Each is obtained by (b) _____

    _____.

6. Three F ratios are then determined, for (a) _____, _____,

    and _____, each obtained by dividing (b) _____ by

    (c) _____.

7. Each F is evaluated by finding in the F table the (a) _____ value of F for the

    given α that is associated with the (b) _____ for the (c) _____

    and (d) _____ of the F ratio.

Answers

1. (a) factorial   (b) 3 X 2   (c) 6   2. (a) two-way   (b) main effects   (c) the A groups
(ignoring variations in B) all come from populations with the same mean   (d) the main effects of
variable B   (e) the B groups (ignoring variations in A) all come from populations with the same
mean   (f) interaction   (g) variables A and B combine additively to affect the dependent
variable (when plotted, the curves of the mean for the A and B groups are parallel)
3. (a) total   (b) SS_{wg} and SS_{bg} (c) one-way   (d) between groups   (e) SS_A, SS_B, and $SS_{A \times B}$
(f) A and B   (g) interaction   (h) $SS_{A \times B} = SS_{bg} - SS_A - SS_B$ 4. (a) number of A groups minus
one   (b) number of B groups minus one   (c) $(df_A)(df_B)$ or (A groups – 1) (B groups – 1)
(d) between groups   (e) $N - k$, where k = total number of groups   (f) between groups and within

groups   5. (a) mean squares (MS's)   (b) dividing each SS by its df 6. (a) the A variable,
B variable and A X B interaction   (b) each MS (MS_A, MS_B, $MS_{A X B}$)   (c) MS_{wg} 7. (a) critical
(b) df's   (c) numerator   (d) denominator

III. CALCULATIONAL PROBLEMS

A 2 X 3 factorial experiment was performed in which there were two conditions for variable A and three conditions for variable B. The N was 15 per group. Some of the SS's are shown in the table below.

1. Complete the ANOVA and fill in the remaining entries in the summary table.

Source	SS	df	MS	F
Variable A	41	___	___	___
Variable B	113	___	___	___
Interaction (A X B)	___	___	___	___
Between groups	182	___		
Within groups	___	___	___	
Total	955	___		

2. Assess the significance of each F, stating the df's and the critical values of F.

3. What conclusion do you reach about each H_0?

4. Estimate effect size for each main effect and the interaction.

Answers

1.

Source	SS	df	MS	F
A	41	1	41	4.46
B	113	2	56.5	6.14
A X B	28	2	14	1.52
Between	182	5		
Within	773	84	9.2	
Total	955	89		

2. For 1 and 84 df, $F_{.05} = 4.00$ and $F_{.01} = 7.08$; the main effects of A are significant at the 5% level. For 2 and 84 df, $F_{.05} = 3.15$ and $F_{.01} = 4.98$. The main effects for variable B are significant at the 1% level; the A X B interaction is not significant.

3. The null hypothesis that the population means for variable A and the population means for variable B are equal are both rejected; it is concluded that each variable significantly affected the dependent variable. The null hypothesis that variables A and B combine additively cannot be rejected.

4.   Variable A: $\hat{\omega}^2 = \dfrac{41 - (1)(9.2)}{955 + 9.2} = \dfrac{31.8}{964.2} = .03$

       Variable B: $\hat{\omega}^2 = \dfrac{113 - (2)(9.2)}{964.2} = .10$

       A X B: $\hat{\omega}^2 = \dfrac{28 - (2)(9.2)}{964.2} = .01$

Name_____   Instructor_____

Date_____

IV.   FURTHER EXERCISES

In problems 1–4, a table is shown that reports the $\bar{X}$'s obtained from an experiment employing a two-way factorial design. In each problem, do the following:

(a) Find the row and column $\bar{X}$'s and enter your answer at the appropriate place in the table. (Assume equal N's per group so that these means can be found by adding up the $\bar{X}$'s in a given row or column and dividing by their number.)

(b) Plot the results of the experiment in a single graph, modeled after Figures 13.1–13.3 in the text. For uniformity, show the B conditions along the baseline.

(c) After inspecting the graph and the two-way table, state whether each F would probably be significant or nonsignificant if a two-way ANOVA were performed.

(d) Based on your inspection of the graph and the conclusions reached in (c), describe the effects of the independent variables and their interaction, referring to the specific conditions employed in the experiment.

1. In a study of helping behavior, students were asked to report to the laboratory either alone, with one other student, or with two other students of the same sex. There were thus 3 types of groups, consisting of one, two, or three participants. Half of each type were male and half were female. The student or students were seated in a waiting room, with the door closed while the experimenter purportedly went to another room to get some equipment. Several minutes later, there was a crash in the hall, followed by the sound of a person moaning. (This accident was staged.) The time taken by someone in the waiting room to open the door and look into the hall was determined. The means for males and females in each group size are shown below.

Sex (variable A)	Size (variable B)			$\bar{X}_A$
	One	Two	Three	
Men	1	5	11	_____
Women	4	7	12	_____
$\bar{X}_B$	_____	_____	_____	

151

(b) Graph of $\bar{X}$'s

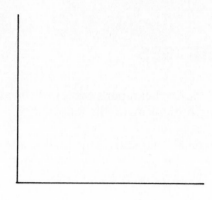

(c) Significance of findings (sig or ns)

Main effects of sex _____   Main effects of size _____   Interaction _____

(d) Description of results

2. In an animal study of the effects of a tranquilizer on emotionality, each subject (a white rat) was placed in a small compartment with a metal grid floor and a lever protruding from one wall. Periodically, a buzzer was sounded and at the same time, the grid floor was electrically charged. The charge was turned off when the animal depressed the lever (which the animals quickly learned to do). Subjects were given 15 trials, half receiving a very mild shock through the grid floor and the other half a stronger one. The next day, 10 extinction trials were given, on each of which the buzzer sounded but was not accompanied by shock. Before the extinction trials, one third of the animals in each of the training shock groups were given a high dosage of a tranquilizer, and another third a low dosage. The remaining third served as a control group, receiving nothing. The time between onset of the buzzer and pressing of the lever was recorded for each subject on the 10th extinction trial as a measure of the amount of emotionality elicited by the buzzer. (Low scores indicate greater emotionality.)

(a)

		Shock (A)	Dosage (B)			
			Control	Low	High	$\bar{X}_A$
	Weak		8	12	14	_____
	Strong		4	7	9	_____
	$\bar{X}_B$		_____	_____	_____	

152

(b) Graph of $\bar{X}$'s

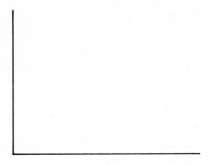

(c) Significance (sig or ns)

Main effects of shock _____   Main effects of dosage _____   Interaction _____

(d) Description of results

3. A psychologist interested in techniques of persuasion presented subjects with a public policy issue about which they had previously indicated they had formed a fairly definite opinion. One half of the subjects were presented with a relatively trivial issue and the other half with a very important one. Members of each group listened to one of two tape-recorded speeches arguing in favor of a position that was contrary to the subject's. One of these messages was couched in strong terms and the other was well-reasoned but low key. After listening to the speech, subjects rated their degree of agreement with the speaker's opinion, on a rating scale running from –3 (strong disagreement) to +3 (strong agreement).

(a)

Issue (A)	Speech (B)		
	Strong	Low Key	$\bar{X}_A$
Trivial	1.2	–1.8	_____
Important	–2.3	.9	_____
$\bar{X}_B$	_____	_____	

(b) Graph of $\bar{X}$'s

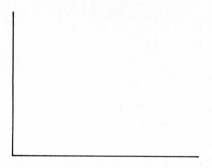

(c) Significance (sig or ns)

Main effects of issue _____ Main effects of speech _____ Interaction _____

(d) Description of results

4. An investigator was interested in demonstrating whether beliefs can bring about distortions in reporting. After giving a questionnaire to students about the existence of extrasensory perception (ESP), he asked students who were strongly convinced and students who were uncertain about the existence of the phenomenon to serve in a study of ESP. Each subject was told that a sealed envelope, held by the experimenter, contained a sheet of paper with a column of 50 letters, each of these 50 letters being one of the first 5 letters of the alphabet. The subject's task was to try to form a mental image of each letter and to write it down on a numbered answer sheet next to the appropriate number (first letter, second letter, and so forth). After the subject completed the task, the experimenter read aloud a list of 50 letters, asking the subject to check off and then to total up his or her correct guesses. For half the subjects in each group, the sealed envelope actually contained the described list and the experimenter read from this list (True condition). For the other half, the envelope was empty and the experimenter read the "correct" letters from a list he surreptitiously selected at random from a stack (False condition). The data were the number of correct guesses shown on the subject's self-corrected answer sheet.

(a)

Condition (A)	Belief (B)		$\bar{X}_A$
	Convinced	Uncertain	
True	12.2	10.1	_____
False	12.5	9.9	_____
$\bar{X}_B$	_____	_____	

154

(b) Graph of $\bar{X}$'s

(c) Significance of results

Main effects of condition _____   Main effects of belief _____   Interaction _____

(d) Description of results

The following problems require computation of a two-way ANOVA. To shorten the calculations, round off SS's to the nearest whole number, MS's to the first decimal place, and F's to the second decimal place. Place the results of your ANOVA in a summary table. Show which F's are significant and at what level. Based on these results, describe the outcome of the study.

5. In a study of "illusory correlations," subjects were given a booklet of 100 pages, each page with a single word typed on it. Each of 10 different words appeared 10 times in random order in the booklet. Nine of the words varied in familiarity from high to low. For one group, the tenth ("target") word was relatively familiar. For the second group, it was low in familiarity and for a third, it was high in familiarity. After reading the word on each page of the booklet, subjects were given the "target" word and asked to estimate how many times (out of 100) it had appeared. Before starting the experiment, half of the subjects had been told that they would be asked to estimate the frequency of appearance of one of the 10 words (but not which word). The other half were simply told to read each word. The sum and sum of squares of the raw scores for each group are shown below. Ten subjects were in each group.

	Familiarity					
	Low		*Medium*		*High*	
	Instr.	No Instr.	Instr.	No Instr.	Instr.	No Instr.
ΣX	91	77	98	100	108	134
ΣX^2	841	613	1012	1012	1196	1822

N = 10 per group

6. Normal individuals and individuals who have a long history of excessive consumption of alcohol were shown a series of word pairs, one member of each pair naming an animal. For each pair, half of the subjects were instructed to press as quickly as possible one of two side-by-side buzzers to indicate whether the animal name was on the right or on the left. The other half of the subjects were instructed to press the buzzer indicating the position of the word that did *not* name an animal. The subjects' reaction times are shown below. The investigator hypothesized that the alcoholics would exhibit a cognitive deficit, particularly on the "not animal" task.

	Normal		Alcoholic	
Animal	Not Animal	Animal	Not Animal
18	24	25	22
23	19	19	29
28	25	22	37
21	30	31	24
25	26	26	35

Section R

Problems for Chapter 14:
Chi Square

I.   TERMS AND SYMBOLS TO REVIEW

Observed frequency (O)   A priori hypothesis
Expected frequency (E)   Test of independence
Chi square (χ^2)

II. SHORT-ANSWER QUESTIONS

1. The chi-square technique is applied to (a) _____ data in which individuals
   are assigned to one of (b) _____ mutually exclusive
   (c) _____.

2. When members of a sample are assigned to one of a single set of categories, χ^2 is used to test an
   a priori hypothesis about the (a) _____ falling into each
   category and therefore what frequencies are (b) _____ in the
   sample. If the hypothesis states that an equal proportion of the population falls into each
   category, this is a hypothesis of (c) _____. Chi square involves
   determining the discrepancy between (d) _____.
   The number of degrees of freedom (df), with one set of categories, is equal to
   (e) _____.

3. Use of χ^2 requires that certain conditions must be met. These include: (1) χ^2 can be used only with (a) _____ data; (2) the individual events or observations must be (b) _____ of each other; (3) unless there is a fairly large number of cells, no (c) _____ frequency should be less than (d) _____; (4) there must be some rational a priori basis for (e) _____; (5) the sum of the expected frequencies and of the theoretical frequencies must be (f) _____.

4. When χ^2 is used to test the significance of the difference between groups, it is called a test of (a) _____. The null hypothesis that is tested is that (b) _____ _____. In this test, $df =$ (c) _____.

5. When two or more groups of individuals differing on some characteristic are selected and then members of the groups are classified on a second categorical variable, the chi-square test of independence applied to the data is called a test of (a) _____ between (b) _____.

6. When a single group of people is selected and each person is then classified according to two categorical variables, the chi-square test of independence applied to the data is called a _____ test.

7. When the number of groups and categories results in df of more than 30, χ^2 can be converted into a (a) _____ and its significance assessed by consulting the (b) _____.

In the following situations, identify whether a test of an a priori hypothesis is called for by stating the expected frequencies or whether a test of independence (Ind) is called for. In the latter case, specify whether it is a test of homogeneity or contingency.

8. An investigator questions a sample of 20 boys and a sample of 20 girls enrolled in a "progressive" nursery school in which gender distinctions are minimized about which of two toys each child prefers: a tea set or a set of tools.

_____

9. A company claims that in its deluxe nut mixture, 30% of the nuts are peanuts, 45% are cashews, and 25% are almonds. A curious consumer buys several jars, consisting of a total of 600 nuts, and decides to test the claim.

_____

10. A debate is going on in a midwestern state about passing a law requiring that "creation science" be taught in biology classes along with the theory of evolution. To determine whether education is related to opinion on the issue, a public opinion pollster questions a sample of voters about whether they are in favor or not in favor of the law and whether they had a high school education or less or more than a high school education.

_____

11. A group of 30 college students are shown a pair of photographs of male students' faces that are very similar except that one of the men is wearing glasses and the other man is not. The subjects are asked which man is more studious. Does the presence or absence of glasses have an effect?

Answers

1. (a) frequency (or categorical)   (b) two or more   (c) categories   2. (a) proportion in the population   (b) theoretically expected   (c) equal likelihood   (d) observed and expected frequencies   (e) number of categories minus one   3. (a) frequency (categorical)
(b) independent   (c) theoretical   (d) 5   (e) setting up the categories   (f) the same
4. (a) independence   (b) one method of classification is unrelated to the other method of classification   (c) (number of row categories minus one) (number of column categories minus one)
5. (a) homogeneity   (b) preexisting groups   6. contingency   7. (a) z score   (b) normal curve table   8. Ind: homogeneity   9. Expected frequencies: 180 peanuts, 270 cashews, 150 almonds   10. Ind: contingency   11. Expected frequencies: 15 and 15

III.   FURTHER EXERCISES

1.   A candy manufacturer makes mints in three colors (white, green, and pink) that are otherwise identical in appearance. The marketing director was interested in whether color affects attractiveness. Three bowls of mints, one of each color, were placed in a restaurant lobby, and the number of customers who helped themselves to each bowl over a 2-hour period was recorded. The frequencies were 24 white, 22 green, and 14 pink. Was there a significant difference in preferences?

2.   In a certain school district, the ethnic breakdown for children enrolled in public elementary schools is 15% black, 9% Hispanic, 6% other minorities, and 70% majority-group white. In one elementary school of 500, the numbers are 62 black children, 33 Hispanic, 24 other, and 381 white. Does the ethnic composition of this school differ significantly from the district as a whole?

3.   In a study of fear of strangers, 20 infants who were 3 months old and 20 infants who were 9 months old were picked up from their cribs by a person they had never seen before. Whether or not the baby cried was recorded, with the results below. Determine whether crying was related to age.

Age	Cried	Did Not Cry	Total
3 months	5	15	20
9 months	13	7	20

(a) In answering the question, compute χ^2 by Formula 14.1.

(b) Compute χ^2 by Formula 14.4 Check to see that the result is the same as in (a).

4. In a cross-national study of male workers, the men's occupations are classified into one of six categories. Data are obtained from samples in 12 countries. A χ^2 is computed to determine whether or not the countries differ in the proportion of men whose occupations fall into each category. Chi square turns out to be 113. Is it significant?

Section S

Problems for Chapter 15:
Nonparametric Techniques

I.   TERMS AND SYMBOLS TO REVIEW

Distribution-free test   Wilcoxon signed-ranks test

Nonparametric test   Friedman two-way analysis

Median test   of variance by ranks

Mann-Whitney U test   Relative efficiency

Kruskal-Wallis one-way   Asymptotic relative efficiency

   analysis of variance by ranks   (ARE)

II.   SHORT-ANSWER QUESTIONS

1. Statistical tests, such as t or F in analysis of variance, that require the estimation of at least
    one population parameter are known as (a) _____ tests. Techniques whose
    theory makes no use of population values are known as (b) _____
    tests. These techniques are also called distribution-free tests because, in contrast to
    parametric tests, (c) _____
    _____.

2. Chi square is an example of a _____ test.

3. The median test with two independent samples is parallel to the parametric technique,
   (a) _____. In this test, members of the two samples
   are classified as falling above or below the (b) _____ of the total
   group. The null hypothesis is then tested that (c) _____
   _____.
   This hypothesis is tested by computation of (d) _____ with $df =$
   (e) _____.

4. Another nonparametric test used to compare two independent groups is
   (a) _____. If the original raw scores are numerical
   data, these scores are first converted into (b) _____. A U statistic is
   computed that is then converted into a (c) _____ score. When N is 8 or more,
   (d) _____ values are used to evaluate the significance of this score.

5. Two nonparametric techniques are parallel to one-way analysis of variance for independent
   groups. One of these tests is the (a) _____ which requires
   computation of the chi square to test the hypothesis that (b) _____
   _____.
   The second is the (c) _____
   _____
   which is an extension of the (d) _____ test and involves
   computation of the (e) _____ statistic.

6. When matched pairs of individuals are tested (or two measures are obtained from the same
   individual), two nonparametric tests that may be used to compare the distributions are the
   (a) _____ test and the (b) _____
   _____.

7. The Friedman test is more flexible than the Wilcoxon because _____
   _____.

8. When the assumptions of parametric tests are met they are preferable to nonparametric tests
   because they _____.

9. The *relative efficiency* of two tests is defined as (a) _____
   _____
   _____.
   If two tests are equally efficient, the relative efficiency is equal to (b) _____.
   Asymptotic relative efficiency (ARE) is the efficiency attained when (c) _____
   _____
   _____.

1. (a) parametric   (b) nonparametric   (c) they make less restrictive assumptions about the shape of the population distribution   2. nonparametric test   3. (a) independent groups t (b) median   (c) the medians of the populations from which the samples were drawn are the same (d) chi square   (e) 1   4. (a) Mann-Whitney U   (b) ranks   (c) z (d) normal curve 5. (a) median test   (b) all the population medians are the same   (c) Kruskal-Wallis one-way analysis of variance by ranks   (d) Mann-Whitney U   (e) H   6. (a) and (b) Wilcoxon signed-ranks, Friedman two-way analysis of variance by ranks   7. any number of matched groups may be compared   8. ordinarily have more power to detect a false H_0 9. (a) the ratio of sample sizes required by each test to obtain the same power value   (b) 1.00   (c) N is sufficiently large that relative efficiency remains relatively constant with further increases in N

III.   CALCULATIONAL PROBLEMS

1.   Two random groups of 8 individuals each were tested under two different conditions, with the results shown below. For the total group of 16, the median score is 18 and the groups are to be compared by the median test.

Group 1	Group 2
3	13
5	16
7	19
10	25
15	28
17	30
20	31
21	32

(a)   Set up a table showing the number in each group at or above the median and below the median.

(b)   The next step is to compute χ^2. Specify the hypothesis that you will test.

(c) Enter the expected frequencies, according to H_0, in the table in (a).

(d) Determine χ^2 and df.

$$\chi^2 \underline{\hspace{2cm}}$$
$$df \underline{\hspace{2cm}}$$

(e) What do you conclude about the effects of the two conditions?

2. Compute a Mann-Whitney U test for the data reported in problem 1.

(a) Determine the ranks for the total set of scores, enter the appropriate ranks next to each score in problem 1, and find the sum of the ranks for each group.

(b) Compute U_1.

$$U_1 \underline{\hspace{2cm}}$$

(c) Compute z.

$$z \underline{\hspace{2cm}}$$

(d) What do you conclude about the effects of the two conditions?

3. Three random groups of 5 each are tested under different experimental conditions. Analyze the data by means of Kruskal-Wallis one-way analysis of variance by ranks.

Group 1	Group 2	Group 3
42	48	61
45	55	65
46	60	68
51	63	69
57	66	71

(a) Assign ranks to the total group of 15 and find the sum for each group. Be sure to give the *lowest* score the rank of 1.

(b) Compute H.

H _____

(c) When sample N's are five or more, H takes the form of the chi-square distribution. What do you conclude about the effects of the experimental conditions?

4. Nine subjects were tested twice, once under each of two experimental conditions, with the following results.

Subject	Condition 1	Condition 2
1	23	26
2	25	24
3	29	31
4	33	34
5	35	40
6	39	37
7	41	43
8	44	45
9	46	49

Compare the two distributions by means of the Wilcoxon signed-ranks test.

(a) Enter the difference (D) scores, absolute ranks, and signed ranks at the right of the scores listed above.

(b) Determine whether performance differed significantly under the two conditions.

5. Six subjects were tested under each of three conditions. Compare the distributions by means of the Friedman two-way analysis of variance by ranks.

Subject	I	II	III	Row Ranks
1	20	23	29	
2	33	35	37	
3	29	27	26	
4	21	25	26	
5	30	32	29	
6	28	29	32	

(a) Rank the three scores of *each subject*, entering the ranks at the right of the list of scores. Then sum the rank for each of the three distributions.

(b) Determine χ^2.

χ^2 _____

(c)　What do you conclude about the effect of conditions?

Answers

1. (a)

	At or above Mdn	Below Mdn	Total
Group 1	2 (4)	6 (4)	8
Group 2	6 (4)	2 (4)	8
Total	8	8	16

(b) H_0: the two populations have the same Mdn.　　(c) see part (a) above　　(d) $\chi^2 = (2-4)^2/4 +$ $(6-4)^2/4 + (6-4)^2/4 + (2-4)^2/4 = 4.00$, $df = (2-1)(2-1) = 1$　　(e) with 1 df, $\chi^2_{.05} = 3.84$. H_0 is rejected; it is concluded that the population medians differ.

2. (a) For Group 1, the ranks are 1, 2, 3, 4, 6, 8, 10, 11, respectively, and $\Sigma R_1 = 45$. For Group 2, the ranks are 5, 7, 9, 12, 13, 14, 15, 16, respectively, and $\Sigma R_2 = 91$.　　(b) $U_1 = (8)(8) + 8(8+1)/2 - 45 = 55$. (c) $U_E = (8)(8)/2 = 32$; $\sigma_U = \sqrt{(8)(8)(8+8+1)/12} = 9.52$; $z = (55-32)/9.52 = 2.42$.　　(d) Obtained z is significant at the 5% level. It is concluded that the conditions had an effect.

3. (a) Group 1 ranks are 1, 2, 3, 5, 7, and $\Sigma R_1 = 18$; Group 2 ranks are 4, 6, 8, 10, 12, and $\Sigma R_2 = 40$; Group 3 ranks are 9, 11, 13, 14, 15, and $\Sigma R_3 = 62$.　　(b) $H = 12/(15)(15+1)[18^2/5 + 40^2/5 + 62^2/5] - 3(15+1)$ $= 9.68$.　　(c) With $df = 3-1 = 2$, $\chi^2 = 5.99$. Calculated H is significant at the 5% level and it is concluded that the groups differ.

4. Difference (D) scores are –3, 1 –2, –1, –5, 2, –2, –1, –3.　　(a) The signed ranks of these D's are –7.5, 2, –5, –2, –9, 5, –5, –2, –7.5. The sum of the positive ranks is 7 and the sum of the negative ranks is –38.　　(b) With $N_{S-R} = 9$, a T value of 6 *or less* is required at the 5% level (Table J). The calculated T of 7 is not significant; it cannot be concluded that the groups differ.

5. (a) For subject 1, the ranks are 1, 2, 3, and so forth. The sums for the distributions are 9, 13, and 14. (b) $\chi^2 = [12/(6)(3)(3+1)][9^2 + 13^2 + 14^2] - 3(6)(3+1) = 2.33$　　(c) For $df = 3-1 = 2$, $\chi^2_{.05} = 5.99$. The calculated value is not significant at the 5% level; it cannot be concluded that the groups differ.

III.   FURTHER EXERCISES

1. Two groups of college students, classified as extroverts or introverts by means of a personality test, were asked to list the names of their friends. The numbers listed by each individual are shown below:

Extroverts	Introverts
3	1
4	2
6	2
7	2
9	3
12	3
14	4
14	6
15	7
16	8

(a) What assumption(s) of random groups t appear to be violated?

(b) Compare the two distributions by means of a median test. (Determine the median by the middle case method.) What do you conclude?

2. Groups of 5-year-old and 8-year-old children were given a probability learning task in which they were asked to guess which of two lights, red or green, would come on next. The red light was shown on 70% of the trials and the green light on 30% of the trials, in a random sequence. On the last 20 trials, the number of guesses of "red" was determined for each child, as shown below. Compare the groups by Mann-Whitney U. What do you conclude?

5 years	8 years
18	16
19	14
20	19
19	15
18	18
20	13
15	13
20	14
19	

3. Laboratory rats prefer and will drink more water flavored with saccharin than plain water. In a study on taste threshold, 3 groups of thirsty rates were allowed to drink from bottles containing either plain water, water with a minute amount of saccharin, or water with a slightly stronger solution. The amount each animal drank in 5 minutes was determined. The results are shown below. Compare the three distributions by means of the Kruskal-Wallis test. What do you conclude about the animals' ability to detect the taste of the saccharin?

Group 1	Group 2	Group 3
Water	Weak	Stronger
13	15	16
12	14	15
10	13	14
9	11	12
7	8	11
7	7	10

174

4. In a study of auditory perception, each of 30 subjects heard material to be identified under two listening conditions. The conditions were compared by means of a Wilcoxon signed-ranks test. The number of signed ranks turned out to be 27 and T turned out to be 150. Complete the analysis.

5. Ten pairs of laboratory rats, each pair from the same litter, were used in an experiment on the effect of a lesion in a certain part of the brain on prior learning. First, all animals were trained in a straight alley in which they were placed in a start box and allowed to run down the alley to a goal box containing food. Running time was recorded. For one member of each pair, an operation was performed in which a small portion of the brain was destroyed (Experimental group). The other animals had a sham operation (Control group). After a lapse of time during which they recovered from surgery, all animals were given 10 additional trials in the straight alley. Total running times are shown below. Perform a Wilcoxon signed-ranks test for the data. What do you conclude?

Pair	Exp.	Control
1	14	10
2	23	20
3	26	19
4	19	21
5	15	9
6	19	14
7	37	38
8	16	13
9	22	20
10	31	24

175

6. A child psychologist has devised a behavior modification program to be applied by parents whose young children frequently throw temper tantrums. He asks parents to record the number of tantrums exhibited by their children for a period of one week during which they are being trained in how to treat their children, for another week 1 month later, and a final week 6 months later. The following results are obtained from 6 children. Compare the distributions by the Friedman two-way analysis of variance by ranks. What do you conclude?

Child	I	II	III
1	18	8	2
2	17	6	0
3	13	14	3
4	11	3	4
5	11	10	5
6	16	9	10

Section T

Special Review:
More on Determining the Appropriate Statistical Test

In the last special review you were given practice in selecting the appropriate statistical test to answer the research question of specific investigations by using the decision tree presented in Chapter 16 of the text and reproduced in Section U of the *Workbook*. By this time, there are several additional kinds of statistical tests that you know how to conduct: one-way and two-way analysis of variance, the χ^2 test of a hypothesis about population proportion or frequencies, and the χ^2 test of independence. In this review, examples of data requiring the use of these techniques are first presented, together with an explanation of how the decision tree is applied to each of them. You are then given a series of practice problems that include all the statistical techniques to which you have been introduced through Chapter 14 (Chi Square) of the text.

Following these problems is a set of problems in which assumptions underlying the use of a parametric test are violated. You are asked to select the nonparametric technique from among those discussed in Chapter 15 that should be used instead. (Parallel parametric and nonparametric tests are listed following the decision tree in Section U.)

Example 1.   The dietician at a summer camp believes that the campers equally prefer white milk and chocolate milk for their midmorning milk and cookies snack. One morning she keeps track of the number of campers who select each type of milk and then uses these data to test her hypothesis.

The decision tree shows us that the first decision to be made is whether the data are numerical or categorical. The answer, of course, is categorical, each child selecting either white or chocolate milk. Thus:

Decision 1: Categorical data.

The second decision, we find from consulting the decision tree, is: How many *sets* of categories? In this example, there is only one set, the preferred type of milk. Thus:

Decision 2: One set of categories.

Plunging on, the third decision is: How many categories within the set? Since there are two kinds of milk, the answer is:

Decision 3: Two categories.

The decision tree indicates that the question calls for a test of a null hypothesis about the proportion in each of the two categories in the population. It further indicates that this H_0 can be tested by either of two tests. A z can be computed about the hypothesized population p (the proportion in the "favored" category), or a χ^2 can be computed using the hypothesized population proportions to determine the theoretically expected frequencies in each category. All that remains is to reread the problem to determine what these population values are hypothesized to be. Since the dietician believes that there is an equal preference, H_0 is that the proportion preferring each color is .50.

Example 2. The same dietician hypothesizes that when given a choice of main course at dinner, 10% of the campers will prefer lamb, 50% will prefer chicken, and 40% will prefer beef. (Obviously, this is an elegant camp, and she wants to order correctly.)

This problem is similar to the previous one in employing one set of categories. Thus:

Decision 1: Categorical data.

Decision 2: One set of categories.

This example differs from the first, however, in the answer to the third decision about the number of categories. Since the choice is lamb, beef, or chicken:

Decision 3: Three categories.

We now know from the decision tree that we are to test an H_0 about population proportions. Since there are more than two categories and the z test is only applicable to a binomial situation, χ^2 must be computed. The hypothesized proportions from which expected frequencies are derived are stated directly in this particular problem (lamb: .10, chicken: .50, and beef: .40).

Example 3. Samples of college seniors majoring in psychology, English, or physics are questioned about whether they have or have not applied to graduate school in their major field. The question is whether differential proportions of students in the three fields currently plan to obtain further graduate training.

Decision 1: Categorical.

Decision 2: Two sets of categories (major and graduate school plans).

The third decision asks: What hypothesis is to be tested? There are two possibilities: a test of a hypothesis about the population proportion in each category, or a test of the hypothesis that one method of classification is unrelated to the other method. In this example:

Decision 3: Classification methods unrelated.

That is, no hypothesis is stated or implied about the specific proportion of seniors in each field who intend to go on to graduate school. Rather, interest is in whether the proportions, whatever they are, are the same or different across field. The specific H_0 to be tested is that they are the same, that is, graduate school plans are unrelated to major. This hypothesis is tested, the decision tree tells us, by a χ^2 test of independence.

Although this is not specified in the decision tree, we can state more exactly that a test of homogeneity among preexisting groups is conducted, using a χ^2 test of independence. That is, three groups of people with different majors were preselected. The question was whether they were alike (homogeneous) in the proportion planning to go on to graduate school.

Example 4. In an exit poll, 200 voters in a city election were asked whether they voted to approve or disapprove a bond issue to finance building new high schools. They were also asked whether they had any children 18 years old or younger, had children older than 18 years, or had no children. The question was whether their status with respect to children was related to their vote on the bond issue.

Decision 1: Categorical data.

Decision 2: Two sets of categories (yes-no vote: no children, children older or younger than 18 years).

Decision 3: Classification methods unrelated.
    The appropriate test is a χ^2 test of independence. More specifically, a contingency test is performed, testing the H_0 that one method of classifying subjects is unrelated to the other method of classification.

Example 5. The relative effectiveness of three methods of teaching children to read is investigated, pupils being compared at the end of the year on a standardized test of reading achievement.

Decision 1: Numerical data (scores on the reading test).

Decision 2: More than two distributions (samples) but only a single variable (teaching method is the only variable, the number of methods being 3).
    We now know that one-way ANOVA is the appropriate technique, testing the H_0 that the three samples come from populations with the same means; that is, children taught by the three methods have the same achievement scores.

Example 6. Another investigator studies the same three methods of teaching reading as in example 5, but selects children from two socioeconomic groups to be taught by each method to determine whether children from different backgrounds react differently.

Decision 1: Numerical data.

Decision 2: Groups classified by two variables (teaching method and socioeconomic status).
    A two-way ANOVA is called for, testing an H_0 about the main effects of variable A, an H_0 about the main effects of variable B (in both instances that population means are all equal), and an H_0 about the A X B interaction—that the variables combine additively.

Practice Problems

    For each of the following examples, determine the statistic to be computed or the statistical test to be conducted. Indicate your answer by choosing the appropriate letter from the following list. Then specify H_0 (if applicable).

(a) χ^2 or z for hypothesis about population p (b) confidence interval for μ (c) t test of hypothesis about μ (d) random groups t test of hypothesis about difference between μ's
(e) matched pairs t test of hypothesis about difference between μ's   (f) Pearson r
(g) Spearman r_s (h) one-way ANOVA   (i) two-way ANOVA   (j) χ^2 test of independence for contingency   (k) χ^2 test of independence for homogeneity of preexisting groups

1. An educational psychologist, interested in effective learning strategies, has college students read a long prose passage for a fixed interval under one of two conditions. In one condition, students were told to underline the most important sentence in each paragraph. In the other condition, subjects were simply asked to read the passage. Subjects were then given an objective test assessing their comprehension of the passage. The investigator predicted that the students asked to underline important sentences would perform better on the comprehension task.

Test (by letter) _____

H_0 (or H_0's) _____

2. In a study of social influence, each subject was asked to judge the length of a series of lines, along with two other subjects. (All subjects were male.) For each line, each subject in turn stated his estimate aloud. Actually, only one of the two was a true subject, the others being the experimenter's confederates who consistently overestimated the length of each line. On 4 of the last 10 lines, the true subject gave his estimate first. For each of these lines, the actual length was subtracted from the subject's estimate. The subject's score was the average amount by which he underestimated or overestimated the lines on these four occasions. Usually there is no systematic error in judging lines so the mean error in groups of subjects is close to zero. The investigator predicted that under the conditions of his experiment, the subjects would tend to overestimate the length of the lines.

Test (by letter) _____

H_0 (or H_0's) _____

3. The organization that has developed a test of scholastic achievement used by colleges to evaluate applicants conducted a study to determine the effects of coaching on test scores. One group was given a review of the type of material covered by the test and experience with practice items for 10 hours during the week before the test. A second group was given the same training, spread out over a month's time. A third group received no coaching.

Test (by letter) _____

H_0 (or H_0's) _____

4. A national company annually hires a large number of recent college graduates as management trainees. At the end of the year, the most successful trainees are promoted to regular management positions and the others are let go. In a study of selection procedures, the personnel director obtains the records of a random sample of 120 trainees hired over the past two years and determines whether their college major was in science, business, education, or liberal arts. The director is interested in finding out whether type of major is related to success as a trainee.

Test (by letter) _____

H_0 (or H_0's) _____

5. In a large national survey of high school students, answers to one of the questions revealed that 45% of the students admitted that they had cheated on an exam at least once. Accepting this figure as a population value, the principal of a local high school gave to 100 students selected at random a questionnaire which was answered anonymously and included a question about cheating. He was curious about whether students at his school were different from students in general.

Test (by letter) _____

H_0 (or H_0's) _____

6. Subjects were presented with a series of pairs of stimuli, some of which consisted of two English words (e.g., house plate) and some of a word and a nonword (e.g., book frune). The subjects' task was to identify which type of pair (two words, one word) was presented as quickly as they could by pressing one of two buttons. The investigator was interested in whether reaction times in identifying the two types of pairs differ.

Test (by letter) _____

H_0 (or H_0's) _____

7. Last year, 8 clinical psychology students in a university's doctoral program took a comprehensive examination which consisted of two parts. The first was an objectively scored written examination assessing their knowledge of the subject matter. The second was an oral examination in which they presented and discussed with the clinical faculty diagnostic and psychotherapeutic protocols of several individuals they had seen in a clinic. At the completion of the oral examination, the faculty decided which student had performed best, worst, and so forth. One of the faculty members decided to find out whether students' performance on the two parts of the exam was related.

Test (by letter) _____

H_0 (or H_0's) _____

8. In a study of the effect of visual cues on memory for spatial order, each subject was seated in a chair, in front of which were five loudspeakers arranged in a semicircle. The subject heard a series of lists of 5 words, each word coming over a different loudspeaker. One third of the subjects were blind, one third were normally sighted but performed the task blindfolded, and one third were normally sighted and not blindfolded. For half the subjects in each group, the first word in each list came from the speaker at the subjects' right, the second from the adjacent speaker, and so forth. For the other half, each word in a list came from a different speaker but the speaker order was not spatially sequential and varied randomly from list to list. After each list was heard, the experimenter stood behind one of the loudspeakers (which varied across lists) and asked which word had been heard through that speaker. Each speaker's number of current responses over the series of lists was determined.

Test (by letter) _____

H_0 (or H_0's) _____

9. A previously unknown Indian tribe has been discovered in a remote area of South America. A physical anthropologist measured the physical characteristics of a sample of tribal members. For example, he measured the heights of adult males, with an eye to setting up a range of values for the mean.

Test (by letter) _____

H_0 (or H_0's) _____

10. Four weeks into their first semester, freshmen were given several questionnaires, one of which determined how lonely they had been feeling since entering college. Another questionnaire assessed their perception of internal versus external locus of control, that is, the degree to which they believed their lives were influenced by their own actions or by other people and situations. The investigator was interested in whether how lonely a student felt was related to the degree to which he or she perceived locus of control to be external, i.e., score on the locus of control questionnaire.

Test (by letter) _____

H_0 (or H_0's) _____

Answers

1. (d), $H_0: \mu_1 - \mu_2 = 0$ 2. (c), $H_0: \mu = 0$ (there is no consistent error of underestimation or overestimation; the conditions of the study had no biasing effect)   3. (h), $H_0: \mu_1 = \mu_2 = \mu_3$
4. (k), H_0: promotion is unrelated to college major; the preexisting groups are homogeneous in promotion   5. (a), $H_0: p_t = .45$ 6. (e), $H_0: \mu_1 - \mu_2 = 0$ 7. (g), (Note that objective test scores would have to be converted to ranks.) If the group is regarded as a random sample from some population, $H_0: r_S = 0$.   8. (i), For speaker order, $H_0: \mu_1 = \mu_2 = \mu_3$; for subject group, $H_0: \mu_1 = \mu_2$; for interaction, H_0: combination is additive   9. (b), H_0: none   10. (f), $H_0: r = 0$

In the following experiments, one or more assumptions of the relevant parametric test are seriously violated. What nonparametric test should be used instead? Make your choice from the list below.

(a) Median test with independent samples (b) Mann-Whitney U for two independent samples (c) Wilcoxon signed-ranks (d) Kruskal-Wallis one-way analysis of variance by ranks (e) Friedman two-way ANOVA

1. Ten elderly residents of a nursing home who had memory problems took a course on memorial strategies to determine whether such a course would lead to improvement. They were tested before and after the course on parallel forms of a memory task. On the first task, most participants had low scores and the group of scores had a small standard deviation. On the second, postcourse task, the standard deviation was much larger.
Test (by letter) _____

2. Lawyers defending a client against a first-degree murder charge prepared three different closing arguments and wanted to know which one would be most persuasive to members of the jury. They hired a pool of individuals, similar in age and other characteristics to the jury, and assigned them randomly to one of three groups. Members of each group read a summary of the evidence and then listened to one of the closing arguments. Finally, without consultation with the others, they filled out a questionnaire asking them how likely they would be to vote for a guilty verdict. The distributions in all three groups were highly skewed.
Test (by letter) _____

3. Physicians often have patients who do not take needed medications, or otherwise do not follow the prescribed course of treatment. A health psychologist on a medical school staff devised a model 4-week training program, designed to increase patient compliance. Fifteen "problem" patients with cardiac heart disease agreed to take part in the program. Their degree of compliance was assessed before the program began, immediately after the program ended, and 3 months later. The distributions differed markedly in variability.
Test (by letter) _____

4. In a project on the antecedents of delinquency, extensive information was obtained on the family background of a group of adolescent boys with a history of antisocial behavior. Similar information was obtained from a group of boys with no history of problem behavior. One item of information was the amount of severe physical and verbal abuse the boys had been subjected to by their fathers when they were 6 years old or younger. Both distributions were nonnormal.
Test (by letter) _____

Answers

1, (c)   2. (a) or (c)   3. (e)   4. (a) or (b)

Section U

Decision Tree

The decision tree presented in Chapter 16 of the text is reproduced in this section. The decision tree outlines a series of questions that you should ask about specific investigations whose answers will ultimately lead you to identify the statistical test that will answer the research question posed by the investigator. The decision tree is limited to the statistical tests discussed in the text through Chapter 14 (Chi Square). The nonparametric tests discussed in Chapter 15 and the parametric tests they parallel are listed at the end of the decision tree.

Practice problems asking you to identify the appropriate statistical test are presented at the end of Chapter 16 in the text and in Sections O and T of this *Workbook*. You might find these problems easier to solve if you tear out the *Workbook* pages on which the decision tree appears so you can consult them without flipping pages back and forth.

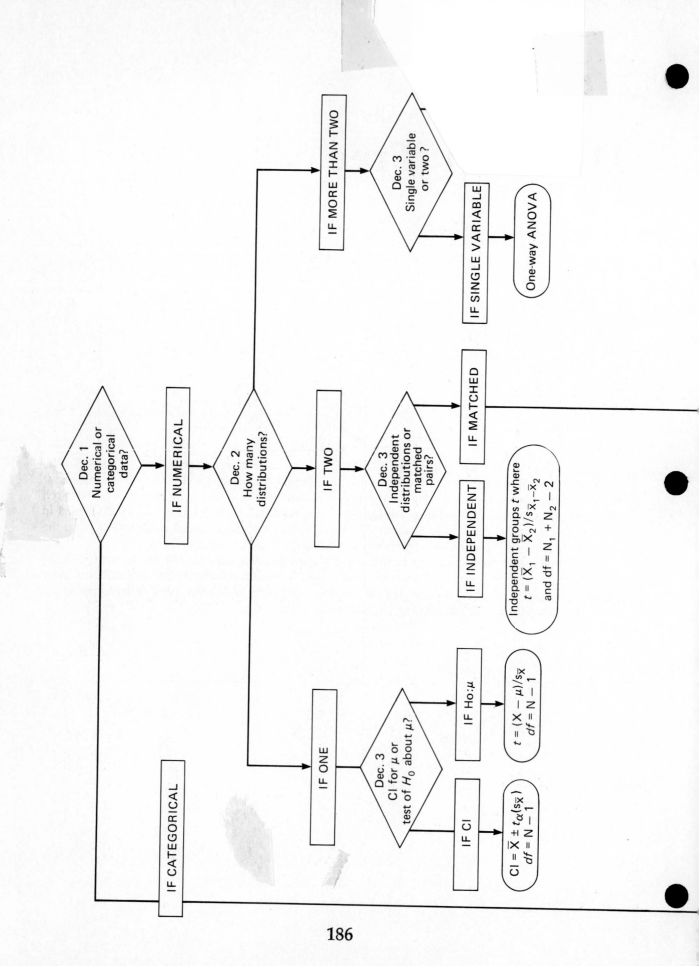

Dec. 1
Numerical or
categorical
data?

IF CATEGORICAL

IF NUMERICAL

Dec. 2
How many
distributions?

IF ONE

Dec. 3
CI for μ or
test of H_0 about μ?

IF CI

CI $= \bar{X} \pm t_\alpha(s_{\bar{X}})$
$df = N - 1$

IF Ho:μ

$t = (X - \mu)/s_{\bar{X}}$
$df = N - 1$

IF TWO

Dec. 3
Independent
distributions or
matched
pairs?

IF INDEPENDENT

Independent groups t where
$t = (\bar{X}_1 - \bar{X}_2)/s_{\bar{X}_1 - \bar{X}_2}$
and $df = N_1 + N_2 - 2$

IF MATCHED

IF MORE THAN TWO

Dec. 3
Single variable
or two ?

IF SINGLE VARIABLE

One-way ANOVA

186

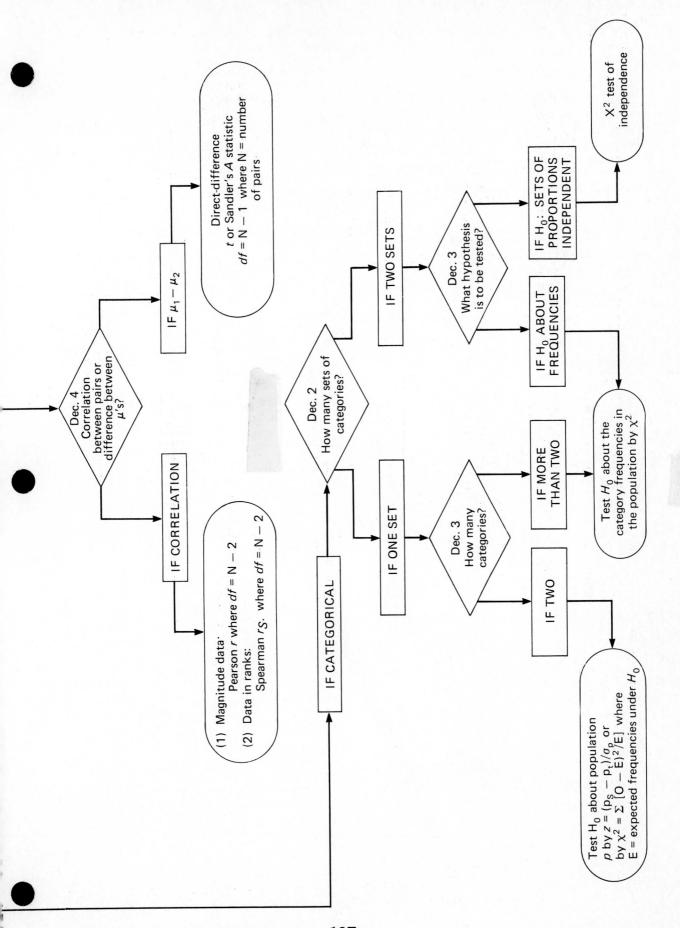

Dec. 4
Correlation between pairs or difference between μ's?

IF $\mu_1 - \mu_2$

Direct-difference t or Sandler's A statistic $df = N - 1$ where N = number of pairs

IF CORRELATION

(1) Magnitude data: Pearson r where $df = N - 2$
(2) Data in ranks: Spearman r_S. where $df = N - 2$

IF CATEGORICAL

Dec. 2
How many sets of categories?

IF TWO SETS

Dec. 3
What hypothesis is to be tested?

IF H_0: SETS OF PROPORTIONS INDEPENDENT

X^2 test of independence

IF H_0 ABOUT FREQUENCIES

IF ONE SET

Dec. 3
How many categories?

IF MORE THAN TWO

Test H_0 about the category frequencies in the population by χ^2

IF TWO

Test H_0 about population p by $z = (p_S - p_t)/\sigma_p$ or by $\chi^2 = \Sigma [O - E]^2/E]$ where E = expected frequencies under H_0

Nonparametric Tests to Use When Assumptions
of Parametric Techniques Are Violated

Parametric Technique	*Parallel Nonparametric Technique*
t-test for comparing $\overline{X}$'s of two independent samples	Median test with two independent samples Mann-Whitney U for two independent samples
t-test for comparing $\overline{X}$'s of two matched samples	Wilcoxon signed-ranks test for two matched samples
One-way ANOVA for independent samples	Median test with more than two independent samples Kruskal-Wallis one-way ANOVA by ranks
One-way ANOVA for matched groups (Note: This technique is not discussed in the text.)	Friedman two-way ANOVA by ranks

Section V

List of Formulas

189

Formula		Text Page
(7.1)	$(p + q)^N = p^N + Np^{N-1}q + \dfrac{N(N-1)}{1 \times 2}p^{N-2}q^2$ $+ \dfrac{N(N-1)(N-2)}{1 \times 2 \times 3}p^{N-3}q^3 + \cdots + q^N$	118
(7.2)	$C_r^N p^r q^{N-r} = \dfrac{N!}{r!(N-r)!}p^r q^{N-r}$	119
(7.3)	$\mu_b = Np$ \qquad (b is the binomial distribution)	121
(7.4)	$\sigma_b^2 = Npq$	121
(7.5)	$\sigma_b = \sqrt{Npq}$	121
(8.1)	$\sigma_{\overline{X}} = \dfrac{\sigma}{\sqrt{N}}$	140
(8.2)	$z = \dfrac{\overline{X} - \mu}{\sigma_{\overline{X}}} = \dfrac{x}{\sigma_{\overline{X}}}$	141
(8.3)	$s_{\overline{X}} = \dfrac{s}{\sqrt{N}}$	142
(8.4)	$t = \dfrac{\overline{X} - \mu}{s_{\overline{X}}}$	144
(8.5)	$df = N - 1$ \qquad (use with Formula 8.4)	150
(8.6)	99% CI for μ: \quad $\overline{X} \pm t_{(.01)}(s_{\overline{X}})$	153
(8.7)	95% CI for μ: \quad $\overline{X} \pm t_{(.05)}(s_{\overline{X}})$	154
(8.8)	$\sigma_{\text{prop}} = \sqrt{\dfrac{p_t q_t}{N}}$	156
(8.9)	$z = \dfrac{p_s - p_t}{\sigma_{\text{prop}}}$	156
(9.1)	$\sigma_{\overline{X}_1 - \overline{X}_2} = \sqrt{\sigma_{\overline{X}_1}^2 + \sigma_{\overline{X}_2}^2}$	169
(9.2)	$z = \dfrac{(\overline{X}_1 - \overline{X}_2) - (\mu_1 - \mu_2)}{\sigma_{\overline{X}_1 - \overline{X}_2}}$	170
(9.3)	$s_{\overline{X}_1 - \overline{X}_2} = \sqrt{s_{\overline{X}_1}^2 + s_{\overline{X}_2}^2}$	170
(9.4)	$t = \dfrac{(\overline{X}_1 - \overline{X}_2) - (\mu_1 - \mu_2)}{s_{\overline{X}_1 - \overline{X}_2}}$	171
(9.5)	$t = \dfrac{\overline{X}_1 - \overline{X}_2}{s_{\overline{X}_1 - \overline{X}_2}}$ \quad where \quad $H_0: \mu_1 - \mu_2 = 0$ \quad and \quad $df = N_1 + N_2 - 2$	172
(9.6)	$s_{\overline{X}_1 - \overline{X}_2} = \sqrt{\dfrac{(N_1 - 1)s_1^2 + (N_2 - 1)s_2^2}{(N_1 + N_2 - 2)}\left(\dfrac{1}{N_1} + \dfrac{1}{N_2}\right)}$	176
(9.7)	$s_{\overline{X}_1 - \overline{X}_2} = \sqrt{\dfrac{(\Sigma X_1^2 + \Sigma X_2^2) - (N_1 \overline{X}_1^2 + N_2 \overline{X}_2^2)}{(N_1 + N_2 - 2)}\left(\dfrac{1}{N_1} + \dfrac{1}{N_2}\right)}$	176
(9.8)	$df = N_1 - 1 + N_2 - 1 = N_1 + N_2 - 2$ \qquad (use with Formula 9.5)	177

191

192

(12.4) $$SS_{tot} = \left(\sum_{tot} X^2\right) - \frac{\left(\sum_{tot} X\right)^2}{N_{tot}}$$ 252

(12.5) $$SS_{bg} = \sum_g \left[\frac{(\Sigma X_g)^2}{N_g}\right] - \frac{\left(\sum_{tot} X\right)^2}{N_{tot}}$$ 252

(12.6) $$SS_{wg} = SS_{tot} - SS_{bg}$$ 253

(12.7) $$SS_{wg} = \sum_g \left[(\Sigma X_g^2) - \frac{(\Sigma X_g)^2}{N_g}\right]$$ 253

(12.8) $$MS_{bg} = \frac{SS_{bg}}{df_{bg}} \qquad \text{where } df_{bg} = k-1 \text{ and } k = \text{number of groups}$$ 256

(12.9) $$MS_{wg} = \frac{SS_{wg}}{df_{wg}} \qquad \text{where } df_{wg} = N_{tot} - k$$ 256

(12.10) $$F = \frac{MS_{bg}}{MS_{wg}}$$ 257

(12.11) $$\hat{\omega}^2 = \frac{SS_{bg} - (k-1)\,MS_{wg}}{SS_{tot} + MS_{wg}}$$ 261

(12.12) $$hsd = q_\alpha \sqrt{\frac{MS_{wg}}{N_g}}$$ 262

(13.1) $$SS_{tot} = \left(\sum_{tot} X^2\right) - \frac{\left(\sum_{tot} X\right)^2}{N_{tot}}$$ 279

(13.2) $$SS_{bg} = \sum_g \left[\frac{(\Sigma X_g)^2}{N_g}\right] - \frac{\left(\sum_{tot} X\right)^2}{N_{tot}}$$ 279

(13.3) $$SS_{bg} = \left[\frac{(\Sigma X_{A1B1})^2 + (\Sigma X_{A1B2})^2 + (\Sigma X_{A1B3})^2 + \cdots + (\Sigma X_{A2B3})^2}{N_g}\right] - \frac{\left(\sum_{tot} X\right)^2}{N_{tot}}$$ 279

where N_g = the number of subjects in each cell

(13.4) $$SS_{wg} = SS_{tot} - SS_{bg}$$ 280

(13.5) $$SS_{wg} = \sum_g \left[(\Sigma X_g^2) - \frac{(\Sigma X_g)^2}{N_g}\right]$$ 280

(13.6) $$SS_A = \frac{(\Sigma X_{A1})^2 + (\Sigma X_{A2}) + \cdots + (\Sigma X_{Am})^2}{N_A} - \left[\frac{\left(\sum_{tot} X\right)^2}{N_{tot}}\right]$$ 280

where N_A = number in each A condition

(13.7) $$SS_B = \frac{(\Sigma X_{B1})^2 + (\Sigma X_{B2}) + \cdots + (\Sigma X_{Bn})^2}{N_B} - \left[\frac{\left(\sum_{tot} X\right)^2}{N_{tot}}\right]$$ 281

where N_B = number in each B condition

(13.8) $$SS_{A \times B} = SS_{bg} - SS_A - SS_B$$ 281

(13.9) $$SS_{A \times B} = N_g \left[\sum_g (\bar{X}_{AB} - \bar{X}_A - \bar{X}_B + \bar{X}_{tot})^2\right]$$ 281

(13.10) $$MS_A = \frac{SS_A}{df_A} \qquad \text{where } df_A = m - 1;$$ 282

$$MS_B = \frac{SS_B}{df_B} \qquad \text{where } df_B = n - 1;$$

$$MS_{A \times B} = \frac{SS_{A \times B}}{df_{A \times B}} \qquad \text{where } df_{A \times B} = (m - 1)(n - 1)$$

$$MS_{wg} = \frac{SS_{wg}}{df_{wg}} \qquad \text{where } df_{wg} = N_{tot} - (m)(n)$$

(13.11) $$F_A = \frac{MS_A}{MS_{wg}} ; \quad F_B = \frac{MS_B}{MS_{wg}} ; \quad F_{A \times B} = \frac{MS_{A \times B}}{MS_{wg}}$$ 283

(13.12) $$\hat{\omega}_E^2 = \frac{SS_E - (df_E)(MS_{wg})}{SS_{tot} + MS_{wg}}$$ 286

(14.1) $$\chi^2 = \Sigma\left[\frac{(O - E)^2}{E}\right]$$ 297

(14.2) df = number of categories – 1   (sample with one-way classification)   298

(14.3) df = (col. – 1)(rows – 1)   (sample with two-way classification)   302

(14.4) $$\chi^2 = \frac{N(AD - BC)^2}{(A + B)(C + D)(A + C)(B + D)}$$ 304

(sample with 2 X 2 classification)

(14.5) $$\frac{x}{\sigma} = \sqrt{2\chi^2} - \sqrt{2n - 1}$$ 306

(15.1) $$U_1 = N_1 N_2 + \frac{N_1(N_1 + 1)}{2} - R_i \qquad \text{(Mann-Whitney U)}$$ 316

(15.2) $$U_E = \frac{N_1 N_2}{2}$$ 316

(15.3) $$\sigma_U = \sqrt{\frac{N_1 N_2 (N_1 + N_2 + 1)}{12}}$$ 316

(15.4) $$z = \frac{U_I - U_E}{\sigma_U}$$ 316

(15.5) $$H = \frac{12}{N(N + 1)} \Sigma\left(\frac{R_i^2}{n_i}\right) - 3(N + 1)$$ 317

(Kruskal-Wallis one-way analysis of variance)

(15.6) $$T_E = \frac{N(N + 1)}{4} \qquad \text{(Wilcoxon signed ranks)}$$ 321

(Friedman two-way analysis of variance)

Summary of Major Formulas

DESCRIPTIVE STATISTICS FOR MAGNITUDE DATA

Mean

$$\bar{X} = \frac{\Sigma X}{N}$$

Standard deviation of sample

$$S = \sqrt{\frac{\Sigma x^2}{N}} = \sqrt{\frac{\Sigma x^2}{N} - \bar{X}^2}$$

Corrected estimate of population SD

$$s = \sqrt{\frac{\Sigma x^2}{N-1}} = \sqrt{\frac{\Sigma X^2 - (\Sigma X)^2/N}{N-1}}$$

z score transformations

$$z = \frac{X - \bar{X}}{s}$$

$$X = \bar{X} + z(s)$$

Standard scores from z scores based on population μ and σ

$$U = (\sigma_U)(z_X) + \mu_U$$

PROBABILITY FOR MUTUALLY EXCLUSIVE EVENTS

Addition rule

$$p(A \text{ or } B \text{ or } C) = p(A) + p(B) + p(C)$$

Multiplication rule, independent events

$$p(A, B, C) = p(A) \times p(B) \times p(C)$$

Multiplication rule, dependent events

$$p(A, B, C) = p(A) \times p(B \mid A) \times p(C \mid A, B)$$

Conditional probabilities

$$p(A \mid B) = \frac{p(A, B)}{p(B)}$$

$$p(B \mid A) = \frac{p(A, B)}{p(A)}$$

PERMUTATIONS AND COMBINATIONS

Permutations

N things N at a time

$$P_N = N! = N(N-1)(N-2) \cdots (1)$$

N things r at a time

$$P_r^N = \frac{N!}{(N-r)!}$$

Combinations

$$C_r^N = \frac{N!}{r!(N-r)!}$$

BINOMIAL DISTRIBUTION

Expression for term in binomial expansion

$$C_r^N p^r q^{N-r} = \frac{N!}{r!(N-r)!} p^r q^{N-r}$$

Mean and SD of binomial

$$\mu_b = Np$$

$$\sigma_b = \sqrt{Npq}$$

t TEST AND CONFIDENCE INTERVALS FOR μ

Estimated standard error of $\bar{X}$

$$s_{\bar{X}} = \frac{s}{\sqrt{N}}$$

t test for H_0 about μ

$$t = \frac{\bar{X} - \mu}{s_{\bar{X}}}$$

where $df = N - 1$

Confidence intervals for μ

99% CI for μ: $\bar{X} \pm t_{(.01)} (s_{\bar{X}})$

95% CI for μ: $\bar{X} \pm t_{(.05)} (s_{\bar{X}})$

z TEST FOR H_0 ABOUT POPULATION PROPORTION

$$z = \frac{p_s - p_t}{\sigma_{\text{prop}}}$$

where $\sigma_{\text{prop}} = \sqrt{\dfrac{p_t q_t}{N}}$

and p_t = proportion in H_0

DIFFERENCE BETWEEN μ_1 AND μ_2 (INDEPENDENT GROUPS)

Estimated standard error of difference

Equal N's

$$s_{\bar{X}_1 - \bar{X}_2} = \sqrt{s_{\bar{X}_1}^2 + s_{\bar{X}_2}^2}$$

Unequal N's

$$s_{\bar{X}_1 - \bar{X}_2} = \sqrt{\frac{(N_1 - 1)s_1^2 + (N_2 - 1)s_2^2}{(N_1 + N_2 - 2)}}$$

$$\times \sqrt{\left(\frac{1}{N_1}\right) + \left(\frac{1}{N_2}\right)}$$

t test for H_0 about difference between μ's

$$t = \frac{\bar{X}_1 - \bar{X}_2}{s_{\bar{X}_1 - \bar{X}_2}}$$

where H_0: $\mu_1 - \mu_2 = 0$ and
$$df = N_1 + N_2 - 2$$

Estimated omega squared

$$\hat{\omega}^2 = \frac{t^2 - 1}{t^2 + df + 1}$$

CORRELATION

Pearson correlation coefficient (r)

Formulas for r

$$r = \frac{\Sigma z_X z_Y}{N}$$

where N = no. of pairs, $df = N - 2$

$$r = \frac{\Sigma XY - \dfrac{\Sigma X \Sigma Y}{N}}{\sqrt{\Sigma X^2 - \dfrac{(\Sigma X)^2}{N}} \; \sqrt{\Sigma Y^2 - \dfrac{(\Sigma Y)^2}{N}}}$$

Prediction of Y from X and X from Y

$$Y_{pred} = r\left(\frac{s_Y}{s_X}\right)X + \bar{Y} - r\left(\frac{s_Y}{s_X}\right)\bar{X}$$

$$X_{pred} = r\left(\frac{s_X}{s_Y}\right)Y + \bar{X} - r\left(\frac{s_X}{s_Y}\right)\bar{Y}$$

Standard error of estimate of X and Y

$$s_{est\,Y} = s_Y\sqrt{1 - r^2}$$

$$s_{est\,X} = s_X\sqrt{1 - r^2}$$

Spearman rank order correlation coefficient

$$r_S = 1 - \frac{6\,\Sigma\,d^2}{N(N^2 - 1)}$$

DIFFERENCE BETWEEN μ_1 AND μ_2 (MATCHED PAIRS)

$$H_0: \; \mu_1 - \mu_2 = 0$$

Direct difference t

$$s_D = \sqrt{\frac{\Sigma D^2 - (\Sigma D)^2/N}{N - 1}}$$

$$s_{\bar{D}} = \sqrt{\frac{s_D{}^2}{N}}$$

$$t = \frac{\bar{D}}{s_{\bar{D}}}$$

where $df = N - 1$

Sandler's A

$$A = \frac{\Sigma D^2}{(\Sigma D)^2}$$

ONE-WAY ANOVA

$$H_0: \; \mu_1 = \mu_2 = \ldots \mu_k$$

Sums of squares

$$SS_{tot} = \left(\sum_{tot} X^2\right) - \frac{\left(\displaystyle\sum_{tot} X\right)^2}{N_{tot}}$$

$$SS_{bg} = \sum_g \left[\frac{(\Sigma X_g)^2}{N_g}\right] - \frac{\left(\displaystyle\sum_{tot} X\right)^2}{N_{tot}}$$

$$SS_{wg} = SS_{tot} - SS_{bg}$$

Mean squares and df's

$$MS_{bg} = \frac{SS_{bg}}{df_{bg}}$$

where $df_{bg} = k - 1$ and k = number of groups

where $df_{bg} = k - 1$ and k = number of groups

Mean squares and df's (continued)

$$MS_{wg} = \frac{S_{wg}}{df_{wg}}$$

where $df_{wg} = N_{tot} - k$

F ratio

$$F = \frac{MS_{bg}}{MS_{wg}}$$

Estimated omega squared

$$\hat{\omega}^2 = \frac{SS_{bg} - (k - 1)\,MS_{wg}}{SS_{tot} + MS_{wg}}$$

hsd follow-up test for pairs of $\bar{X}$'s

$$hsd = q_\alpha \sqrt{\frac{MS_{wg}}{N_g}}$$

TWO-WAY ANOVA

Sum of squares

$SS_{tot}, SS_{bg}, SS_{wg}$ (see one-way ANOVA)

$$SS_A = \frac{(\Sigma X_{A1})^2 + (\Sigma X_{A2})^2 + \cdots + (\Sigma X_{Am})^2}{N_A}$$

$$- \frac{\left(\sum_{tot} X\right)^2}{N_{tot}}$$

where N_A = number in each A condition

$$SS_B = \frac{(\Sigma X_{B1})^2 + (\Sigma X_{B2})^2 + \cdots + (\Sigma X_{Bm})^2}{N_B}$$

$$- \frac{\left(\sum_{tot} X\right)^2}{N_{tot}}$$

where N_B = number in each B condition

$$SS_{A \times B} = SS_{bg} - SS_A - SS_B$$

Mean squares and df's

$$MS_A = \frac{SS_A}{df_A}$$

where $df_A = m - 1$;

$$MS_B = \frac{SS_B}{df_B}$$

where $df_B = n - 1$;

$$MS_{A \times B} = \frac{SS_{A \times B}}{df_{A \times B}}$$

where $df_{A \times B} = (m - 1)(n - 1)$

$$MS_{wg} = \frac{SS_{wg}}{df_{wg}}$$

where $df_{wg} = N_{tot} - (m)(n)$

F ratios

$$F_A = \frac{MS_A}{MS_{wg}}$$

$$F_B = \frac{MS_B}{MS_{wg}}$$

$$F_{A \times B} = \frac{MS_{A \times B}}{MS_{wg}}$$

Estimated omega squared

$$\hat{\omega}_E^2 = \frac{SS_E - (df_E)(MS_{wg})}{SS_{tot} + MS_{wg}}$$

where E = effect being assessed

NONPARAMETRIC TESTS

Chi square

$$\chi^2 = \Sigma \left[\frac{(O - E)^2}{E}\right]$$

df = number of categories – 1
(sample with one-way classification)

200

Mann-Whitney U

$$z = \frac{U_1 - U_E}{\sigma_U} \quad \text{where:}$$

$$U_1 = N_1 N_2 + \frac{N_1(N_1 + 1)}{2} - R_1$$

$$U_E = \frac{N_1 N_2}{2}$$

$$\sigma_U = \sqrt{\frac{N_1 N_2 (N_1 + N_2 + 1)}{12}}$$

Kruskal-Wallis one-way ANOVA

$$H = \frac{12}{N(N + 1)} \Sigma \left(\frac{R_i^2}{n_i} \right) - 3(N + 1)$$

Wilcoxon signed ranks

$$z = \frac{T - T_E}{\sigma_T} \quad \text{where:}$$

$$T_E = \frac{N(N + 1)}{4}$$

$$\sigma_T = \sqrt{\frac{N(N + 1)(2N + 1)}{24}}$$

Friedman two-way ANOVA

$$\chi_R^2 = \frac{12}{Nk\ (k + 1)}\ (\Sigma R_i^2) - 3N(k + 1)$$